NATIVE AMERICAN
WARRIORS

THE LEGENDARY TRIBES, THEIR
WEAPONS AND FIGHTING TECHNIQUES

MARTIN J. DOUGHERTY

amber
BOOKS

Copyright © 2018 Amber Books Ltd

Published by Amber Books Ltd
United House
London N7 9DP
United Kingdom
www.amberbooks.co.uk
Instagram: amberbooksltd
Facebook: www.facebook.com/amberbooks
Twitter: @amberbooks

ISBN 978-1-78274-669-0

Project Editor: Michael Spilling
Designer: Zoë Mellors
Picture Researcher: Terry Forshaw

Printed in UAE

Contents

Introduction

The Native American people have been characterized in many ways – as great hunters, as a deeply spiritual people and of course as legendary warriors. Warfare and conflict were an essential part of their society long before Europeans arrived in the Americas, but did not define the culture of the Native American people.

Their many societies were diverse, complex and highly evolved, and although there were shared characteristics there was no single 'Native American way of life' and few of the common stereotypes really apply. Like most people, the average Native American just wanted to live their life and all but a few viewed conflict as at best a necessary evil. But when the necessity arose they could and would fight very well indeed.

The first encounter Europeans had with Native American warriors was when Norsemen from Greenland attempted to establish a colony in what they called 'Vinland' (now thought to be Newfoundland) around 1000 CE. Vinland had been discovered by Leif Eriksson, whose crew wintered there before sailing back to their homes in Greenland. Eriksson's brother Thorvald next attempted to found a colony on the site of the winter camp.

This might have gone well had the Norsemen treated the local population fairly. However, they viewed the Stone Age indigenous people with contempt, referring to them as Skraelings (wretches) and routinely cheating them in trade. Conflict broke out, and at first the Norsemen were confident in their fortified camp, not least since they possessed the best weapons and armour early medieval Europe could produce.

However, possession of state-of-the-art military equipment did not save Thorvald's expedition. The Norsemen found themselves under virtual siege in their camp by people who were skilled in the hunt and knew the land well. The result was inevitable and in due course the Norsemen returned to Greenland. No further incursions took place for several centuries, although naturally there was conflict between different groups of Native Americans. By the time the next Europeans arrived, both societies were far more advanced than they were in 1000 CE.

ORIGINS OF THE NATIVE AMERICAN PEOPLE

At the height of the Last Ice Age, our world was a very different place. The Last Glacial Maximum occurred around 26,000–27,000 years ago, with considerable amounts of water locked up in the glaciers and ice sheets. This had the effect of lowering sea levels and making large areas of land completely uninhabitable. Around the fringes of the great ice sheets were regions of tundra and other barely habitable terrain, with the surviving human populations forced into warmer areas where food was available. Even here, life was hard. Rainfall was less than in modern times, reducing the ability of the land to support plant and animal life.

This was only part of a larger cycle. Several Ice Ages have occurred during the existence of our planet, and within each there have been warmer periods when the glaciers retreated followed by a return of extensive glaciation. There is little evidence of what sort of societies existed before the beginning of the Ice Age or within the warmer interglacial periods. However, it is known that the people of the Last Glacial Maximum were both anatomically and behaviourally modern humans. Anatomically modern humans appeared around 200,000–300,000 years ago, with behaviourally modern people emerging around 40,000 years ago during the last glaciation. 'Behaviourally modern' in this case

Facing page: Hunting a large animal such as a mastodon with stone-tipped spears required a combination of agility, courage and trust in other members of the hunting party.

Below: The people who drove the Norsemen from the Americas may have been Inuit; the Norse colonists called them by the same name that they used for the Greenland Inuit.

Above: The people of the Clovis era lived in a time when the retreating ice was causing major climatic changes. A nomadic lifestyle was necessary to follow game and other food sources.

Facing page: Archaeological evidence suggests that what is now Maryland may have been inhabited 16,000 or more years ago as humans spread into the region from the southwest.

refers to the existence of language and abstract thought conveyed by art, among other indicators. These people evolved during the glaciation – and quite possibly because of it – and began to spread out when the ice sheets finally began to retreat.

Glaciation did not end quickly or suddenly. Gradual warming led to some melting of the ice sheets, but this was a process requiring thousands of years. Conditions varied from one region to another, with the result that modern scientists typically refer to conditions in a particular region rather than worldwide. Thus in the North American continent this period is known as the Wisconsin Glaciation. Its maximum extent of ice coverage occurred around 21,000–26,000

years ago. One consequence of the glacial maximum was the creation of Beringia, a land bridge between the North American and Asian continents where the modern Bering Strait is located.

Although lying at a very northerly latitude, low snowfall meant that Beringia was not covered in ice and remained habitable, with a similarly ice-free region around each end of the land bridge.

It was through this ice-free zone that humans and many animal species crossed from Asia into the Americas. The first humans to make the crossing would not have realized that they were moving from one continent to another; they were simply following the game available in this relatively welcoming land.

Once in the Americas, the new arrivals found their way was blocked by ice sheets, initially channelling expansion into a few narrow corridors. As the ice sheets retreated, new lands opened up along with the ability to reach other ice-free areas, thus allowing the human population to begin spreading throughout the continent.

The warming of the climate and melting of the ice sheets caused sea levels to rise, eventually inundating most of Beringia and cutting off the land bridge. This ensured there was no further migration into the Americas. The population already established there represented the whole available gene pool and, without further arrivals, would diverge from other human populations over the next few thousand years.

The warming of the climate caused freshwater lakes to form within the ice sheets, which were for the most part trapped by ice dams. When these finally melted, the effect was an outrush of water that ran to the sea and in many cases affected ocean currents. One consequence was a sudden drop in average temperature in the northern hemisphere as the flow of warmer water from the equator was disrupted. The early human population in the Americas was affected by these climate changes as well as dramatic local events caused by the breaking of ice dams, but survived and continued to spread. The climate began to warm once more after around 11,700 years ago, opening up new lands and permitting the spread of humans to the east coast and into the far north and south.

EARLY SETTLEMENT OF THE AMERICAN CONTINENT

There is much debate about whether the American continent was settled by a single large influx of people, possibly two or more such migrations, or perhaps a flow of smaller groups across the Beringia land bridge before it finally closed. Likewise, it is unclear exactly when the first humans arrived in the Americas. New archaeological finds have suggested various dates and cast doubt upon others, but of course the earliest known presence is simply the earliest evidence found – it does not mean that humans were not previously present in numbers too small to make evidence likely to survive. The rise in sea levels accompanying the melting of the ice sheets may have obliterated many early sites.

Facing page: There was nothing
primitive about Clovis spear-points,
other than the materials from which
they were fashioned. Designs were
optimized for the game they were
intended to be used on.

Below: Although often described as
'mammoth hunters', the Clovis-era
people would have taken whatever
game presented itself. A mammoth
represented a great deal of food gained
only at grave risk.

It is possible that human
migration into the American
continent began as early as 20,000
years ago, although more recent
dates are supported by much of the
available evidence. What is known
was that these humans only had
access to Stone-Age technology,
and that their lifestyle was that
of the hunter-gatherer. Although
primitive by many standards, these
people were smart and resourceful,
and were skilled at making stone
tools adapted to their specific
requirements. In this they differed

from earlier humans who had
produced rather basic tools.

This era is generally referred
to as the Upper Palaeolithic;
essentially the last part of the 'Stone
Age'. Craftspeople were capable of
producing quite sophisticated tools
and weapons designed for hunting
and the treatment of hides and
meat obtained from prey animals.
Hunter-gatherers also possessed a
wealth of knowledge about what
food was available when and
where. Barring sudden changes
in local weather and climate

conditions, this knowledge allowed hunters to be in the right place to hunt deer, to take advantage of fish moving upriver to spawn and to find suitable fruit, berries and other plant materials to fit their needs.

Although theirs was a harsh existence, these early Americans knew how to live off the land well enough that despite changing conditions their population gradually grew. As the ice receded and corridors opened up to new lands, these were colonized and

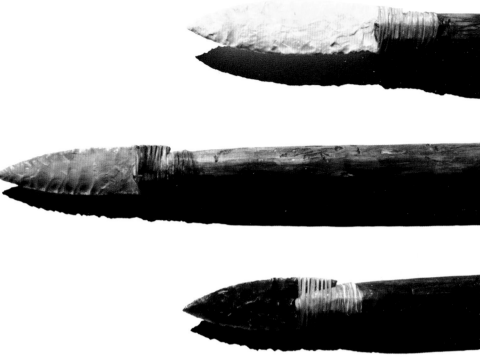

"Although theirs was a harsh existence, these early Americans knew how to live off the land well enough..."

their new opportunities exploited. It is known that by around 13,000 years ago humans had reached what is now New Mexico. Archaeological finds around Clovis in New Mexico dating from this time were for several decades thought to be the earliest indication of human activity in the Americas, although there is now some evidence that may point to earlier – possibly much earlier – habitation.

The Clovis people would obviously have required some time to spread down from Beringia,

and this is unlikely to have taken the form of a direct march as soon as the ice sheets melted sufficiently to permit it. Thus, if there were people in the Clovis region around 13,000 years ago, then it seems likely that humans were present in North America for centuries before that. It may never be proven conclusively whether much older cultures existed, but it is known that at the time of the Clovis people humans were using sophisticated hunting tools.

The spears used by Clovis-era humans had a distinctive

tip, known as a Clovis point. Painstakingly chipped from flint and similar materials, the Clovis spearpoint could be up to 20cm (7.9in) long, and was attached to a wooden haft to make a deadly weapon. Spearpoints from other eras or regions often differ in size and shape from the Clovis designs; it is clear that these people had a specific design that suited their purposes and was probably the result of long experience and practical experimentation.

> "There is considerable evidence that the Clovis-era Native Americans were capable of hunting and killing megafauna such as the mammoth."

There is considerable evidence that the Clovis-era Native Americans were capable of hunting and killing megafauna such as the mammoth, and that this took place on a more or less routine basis. Even with technological assistance such as high-quality stone-tipped spears and mammoth traps in the form of concealed spiked pits, to the modern imagination there can be little 'routine' about puny humans hunting something as huge and dangerous as a mammoth, but it does seem that the Clovis people did so. Indeed, they may have hunted the mammoth to extinction.

Mammoths and other megafauna were under pressure as a result of the changing climate, and it may have been the activities of early hunters that pushed them over the edge. Analysis using software developed to study the impact of human hunting on elephant populations produced results that suggest that human predation – even on the limited scale possible in such primitive conditions – may have been a factor in depleting the North American mammoth population beyond the point where it could recover. There is evidence that the mammoth did not become entirely extinct during the Clovis era but it may well have been driven into a few small survivor populations.

Butchered mammoth remains and Clovis-style stone tools have been found together, suggesting that the people of this era ate the meat of megafauna they had hunted and killed, although in all likelihood they would take easier game when it was available. People capable of sufficient organization, and possessing good enough weaponry, to take a mammoth would be capable of hunting almost any land creature, and of course if they fought one another the same tools and skills would stand them in good stead.

THE PALEO-INDIAN PERIOD

Whether the Clovis people were the first human inhabitants of North America or, as recent evidence suggests, settlement took place earlier than previously thought, there were definitely humans in the Americas around 13,000 years ago. If they had reached New Mexico in sufficient numbers to leave the traces that

we can find today, it seems likely that humans had been expanding across the continent for hundreds of years at least.

This expansion was long believed to have taken place through an ice-free corridor between the Cordilleran ice sheet surrounding the Rocky Mountains and the larger Laurentide ice sheet covering the east of the continent. This theory retains

widespread acceptance, but dating of archaeological sites and new estimates of the timing of ice sheet melting have cast doubt upon overland migration as the means by which Clovis-era humans reached the New Mexico region.

It is possible that movement into the Americas took place along the coasts, either as well as overland or as a sole means of expansion. This theory fits with the

Above: Much of a hunter's work went into preparing his weapons, which could be accompanied by socialising with his family and the rest of the tribe.

Alternative Theories

There are other theories about the spread of humans into the Americas. Some might be politely described as 'wacky' but others are based on scientific evidence – albeit disputed in some cases – and attempt to explain genetic or technological traits observed in early human remains.

It is possible that humans got into the Americas by other routes than a land crossing through Beringia. One theory holds that people might have traversed the southern edge of the Atlantic ice sheet in small boats, going ashore on the ice to hunt or fish. Other theories do not offer a clear-cut explanation of how people arrived there, but suggest that remains found in Central and South America could date from as early as 50,000 years ago.

New evidence will continue to come to light over the years, but it is quite possible that we may never know exactly when humans entered the Americas or how they spread out over time. Some evidence is hotly disputed, with claims that certain sites could date from anything between 10,000 to 50,000 years ago backed up by at least some evidence.

Above: Children learned the skills of the hunt from an early age, and would not be permitted to join a hunting party until they were highly competent.

What does seem certain is that humans were present in the Americas 10,000–15,000 years ago and possibly earlier, and that they developed separately from populations in Europe and Africa, although there may have been some contact with East Asian people until rising sea levels made this impossible.

discovery of pre-Clovis remains to the south of the Clovis sites, although the dating of some of these is controversial. Whatever the means, humans spread out across the continent to create an initially very dispersed population.

The lifestyle of these people would be broadly similar across most of the continent – they were hunter-gatherers capable of making stone tools and using them in inventive ways. There would not be room for much cultural variance at first, but as the groups spread out and became isolated from one another the experiences they had and the conditions they lived in would begin to shape their mindset and beliefs.

This period of settlement and migration followed by establishment of populations in general areas of the American continent is known as the Paleo-Indian era. It came to an end around 9000 years ago, although this is a very general figure and subject to local variations. Sea levels had been rapidly rising as the melting of ice sheets dumped large amounts of water into the oceans, and it may be that as this process tailed off climatic conditions improved sufficiently to permit population expansion and a reduction in the number of potentially catastrophic setbacks encountered by a given regional population.

Left: Bone, wood and stone were the primary materials used by Native Americans until the arrival of Europeans, and remained in more limited use afterward.

"...as the groups spread out and became isolated from one another the experiences they had ... would begin to shape their mindset and beliefs."

Rainfall increased in many areas too, and the levels of dust in the atmosphere were reduced at the same time. The effects seem to have been worldwide, as at around the time the Paleo-Indian era ended in the Americas the cultivation of wheat was beginning in Mesopotamia. A direct connection is rather unlikely; it is more probable that societies worldwide responded to the stabilizing of their environment.

The relatively rapid inundation of low-lying areas and consequent changes in terrain would have made

Above: Petroglyphs have been found in several parts of the North American continent, some dating from prehistoric times and others carved after the arrival of Europeans.

A sudden decrease in temperatures worldwide, known as the 8.2 kiloyear event, took place 8200 years ago – hence its name. This was probably caused by the final collapse of the Laurentide ice sheet, whose remnants contained large meltwater lakes that rushed to the sea once released. The immediate effects would have been serious in the North American continent, and the climatic changes had effects that were felt worldwide.

The people of North America weathered these difficult times and came to dominate the whole continent. Populations began to specialize based on their home area, creating the beginnings of distinct cultures. These populations were not isolated, however; there is evidence of trade between regions and cultural exchange must have taken place. The very different conditions in widely separated parts of the continent was undoubtedly a factor in the development of distinct tribal identities.

THE MESO-INDIAN PERIOD

The Meso-Indian Period is considered to have begun around 8000 years before the present day. Tools were still made of stone, but advances in tool-making created chipped rather than flaked stone tools. Similarly, a variety of hunting techniques and equipment emerged, including the use of nets and fish-hooks. The area a particular group ranged over gradually shrank as a result of improved hunting technique, creating a trend towards a more settled lifestyle.

life difficult for a hunter-gatherer culture and may have forced movement out of a previously fruitful area. As this process slowed, the early tribes would have been able to establish a territory and to depend on the availability of game at predictable times and places. Migration would still have occurred but it was less likely to be dictated by changing conditions.

A nomadic existence was still the norm, but whereas earlier populations might wander over a huge area and never return to the same place twice, the Meso-Indian hunter group would have preferred locations to find game or other food at different times of the year, and having already found a good campsite in that area they would be unlikely to choose not to use it again.

Groups were on the whole small, but there is evidence that sometimes multiple groups would merge for a time or at least live and hunt together. This would

"Groups were on the whole small, but there is evidence that sometimes multiple groups would merge for a time, or at least live and hunt together."

allow ideas to be exchanged and intermarriage to take place between the different groups. Primitive societies worldwide seem to be aware of the dangers of inbreeding and typically avoid it where possible by exchanging tribe

Below: The early Native Americans were inventive, using natural materials to solve problems such as how to efficiently catch fish.

members with other groups when they were encountered.

These nomadic populations left relatively little trace of their existence other than pits used to dispose of bones, shell-middens and similar domestic refuse deposits that modern scientists use to determine population numbers, diet and seasonal movement habits. The North American continent had plenty of useable land and suitable game, and with a small starting population there was no real need for competition over resources.

That is not to say that conflict did not occur – humans have fought one another for the whole of their existence, not always out of necessity. However, for the most part the low population density and ability for a threatened group to find an equally good hunting ground elsewhere meant that conflict and competition was much less than in Europe.

One implication of this dispersed population was reduced pressure to innovate. Technology advanced far more rapidly in Europe than in the Americas, with cities appearing around 6500 years ago. The construction of towns and conurbations depended upon a move from hunting to a farming-based society, and required the solution of various technological problems that further spurred progress among Native Americans.

There was simply no need to adopt this new way of life in the Americas, so while farming was eventually adopted by some cultures there was no powerful incentive to do so. In Europe, the city-building, farming-based societies could support a larger population base than their nomadic neighbours, enabling them to drive off the less developed people from their borders. In short, in Europe and the Middle East the city-builders won the war for resources; in the Americas the war never happened.

Organized states did arise in both Europe and the Americas, in the sense that a large tribe with a cultural identity and willingness to help its members at times of need can be considered a state even if it has no grand capital or walled cities. The tribes and tribal confederations of the Americas developed a sophisticated social system to rival anything seen in Europe, but there was no need for this to happen quickly.

Some American societies built permanent structures even though

Below: The Painted Rock petroglyph site is the largest of over 40 sites near Gila Bend, Arizona. It contains around 800 separate images.

their lifestyle was not sedentary. The earliest known example is Watson Brake in Louisiana. This was a 'mound city', composed of a ring of earth mounds connected by a ridge or bank of earth. Construction began around 5500 years ago, although the site is known to have been in use for centuries before that.

The Watson Brake site is unusual in that it appears to have been built by nomadic people who did not settle down once construction was completed. Other later mound-cities were inhabited on a permanent basis. However, while mound constructions can only take so many forms and therefore tend to be similar, it does appear that mound cities were built for a variety of purposes by different groups, and that not all were designed for habitation.

The construction of these early mound cities presented a significant challenge to a hunter-gatherer culture. Bringing enough people together and supporting them while they worked was

Above: Nomadic hunter-gatherers lived in simple shelters constructed from materials they could carry or rely on obtaining wherever they stopped. Over time, distinct shelter designs appeared.

> "The tribes and tribal confederations of the Americas developed a sophisticated social system to rival anything seen in Europe."

not an easy task for the agrarian societies of Europe and the Middle East. For semi-nomadic hunters it represents an incredible achievement. However, little is known about the culture of this era as no written records as such were left behind. Even big questions such as why the mounds were built remain, for the most part, unanswered. Other aspects of life in this era are better understood.

The stone-tipped spears of the Clovis era were designed for jabbing or throwing over a short distance. While quite capable of taking down a large animal such as a mammoth, this required getting very close and inflicting multiple wounds before the beast was weakened enough to collapse. Even with a team of experienced hunters, some of whom would distract and confuse the prey while others closed in from the flanks to make their attack, taking on large prey was dangerous and smaller animals might escape before the hunters could cast their weapons.

The spear of the Meso-Indian era was shorter, with a variety of head designs. It could be thrown with the assistance of an atlatl, a stick with a hook at one end upon which the base of the spear rested. The atlatl increased the velocity of a spear cast, thereby extending range, accuracy and the chance of bringing down prey.

Below: Petroglyphs at Sand Island in Utah depict, among other creatures, mammoth and bison. This confirms the theory that humans and mammoths co-existed at least for a time.

THE NEO-INDIAN PERIOD

The construction of mound complexes ceased for a time, resuming around 3500 years before the present. Best known of the mound structures of this period is Poverty Point, which was constructed over a period of centuries for unknown purposes. It has been postulated that its earthworks may have had religious significance, or that it may have been a settlement and trading centre.

Archaeologists have named the society that built this structure the Poverty Point culture. Many other mound complexes were built by the same people who lived around the Mississippi but maintained a

system of trade over a much wider area. The Poverty Point culture lasted until about 2700 years before the present day, and was just one of the groupings to arise in the Neo-Indian Period.

Above: A replica Hopewell-era dwelling on display at the Fort Ancient archaeological part in Ohio. The Hopewell culture existed until around 500 CE.

> "It has been postulated that its earthworks may have had religious significance, or that it may have been a settlement and trading centre."

The next society known to have arisen in the same area is the Tchefuncte. While less

Right: The Chillicothe site in Ohio was constructed by the Hopewell culture as a burial site. Other mound complexes in the area may have had different functions.

widespread in terms of trade links, the Tchefuncte people were able to make pottery that permitted improved storage and transportation of food. Preparation of meals was also enhanced, as fired-clay vessels could be used to make stews and other relatively complex dishes. The Tchefuncte people were still hunter-gatherers, building temporary homes wherever they stopped.

Cultural and social development continued. The Tchefuncte culture came to an end around 1800 years ago at a time when the Roman Empire was at its height. The Tchefuncte society was replaced by what modern historians call the Marksville culture after its primary archaeological site in Avoyelles Parish, Louisiana. The Marksville people practised ritual burial, constructing elaborate mound tombs for high-status individuals.

Contemporary with the Marksville culture was the Santa Rosa-Swift Creek culture, which is known to have been able to work copper. To the north, in what is now Ohio and the surrounding area, dispersed populations were linked by an extensive trade network known as the Hopewell culture. This was not a tribe as such; it is better considered as a set of characteristics or social norms exhibited by dispersed groups.

The Hopewell culture was characterized by short-term

HOHOKAM WARE
HOHOKAM/SALADO AREA
AD 700~AD 1300

WHITE MOUNTAIN REDWARE
ANASAZI AREA
AD 1000~AD 1450

EL PASO POLYCHROME
MOGOLLON AREA
AD 1200~AD 1300

Above: The development of pottery was a major step forward for the Native American peoples, allowing new ways of preparing and storing food to be developed.

habitation in an area, using shelters constructed for the purpose, followed by relocation when the need arose. Trade generally followed the rivers, radiating out from settlements that acted as commerce hubs. Goods flowed between these and were then dispersed among the smaller settlements. In this way necessary

or desirable items were traded all the way from the Great Lakes to the Gulf of Mexico.

The most prominent remains of the Hopewell culture are at Chillicothe in Ohio. This is a burial mound complex that was apparently not used as a settlement, whereas other sites were inhabited as well as serving a burial function.

"...art objects have been discovered from these cultures, many of which seem to be associated with spiritualism or shamanism."

ANASAZI WHITEWARE/LINO GREY
& MESA VERDE BLACK-ON-WHITE
ANASAZI AREA
LINO GREY · AD 500 · MESA VERDE B/W · AD 1150

the preceding Adena culture, whose people built hundreds or perhaps thousands of mounds in the period from around 3000 years ago to 2200 years before the present day. Large numbers of art objects have been discovered from these cultures, many of which seem to be associated with spiritualism or shamanism.

It may be that the most important people in the Hopewell culture were interred there, implying that a complex hierarchy existed. This is borne out by other evidence indicating social development beyond the informal organization of typical hunter-gatherer societies.

The Hopewell culture is thought to have developed from

Periods in North American History

The history and prehistory of the North American continent can be grouped into general eras based on observed characteristics. Precise dates for when one era faded into the next are impossible to determine as there are few indicators and no written records. Regional variations also occurred, and differing systems are used to define eras depending on the purpose of the observer.

Paleo-Indian Period: From the first arrival of humans on the continent to around 10,000 years ago. The transition to the Archaic period was triggered by climatic change, and was thus both gradual and uneven. The transition from this era to the next is widely considered to have been on-going until 6000 years before the present day in some areas.

Meso-Indian Period: From the end of the Paleo-Indian period to around 3000 years ago. Alternatively, some observers use the term **Archaic Period**, which is sometimes considered to have spanned the era from the end of the Paleo-Indian period to around 4000–5000 years before the present day.

Neo-Indian Period: From the end of the Meso-Indian Period to the arrival of Europeans in the Americas around 500 years ago. This period is often subdivided into shorter eras based upon local conditions, and is also referred to as the **Formative Period** or the **Woodland Period**. This era is characterized by the development of pottery, the construction of burial mounds and the deliberate cultivation of food plants.

Hunter-Gatherer vs Farmer

There is a natural tendency to assume that a settled, farming-based economy is superior, and that hunter-gatherers were too primitive to embrace this advantage. This is not the case. It takes considerable intellect and resourcefulness to thrive in a nomadic environment, and those who practised this lifestyle were anything but dim-witted.

The hunter-gatherer needed to understand the land and the signs it gave that food (and danger) might be present. Armed with a good working knowledge of animal habits, 'primitive' hunters moved to where game animals would appear at that time of year then positioned themselves to ambush their prey. They knew how best to hunt different types of animal and where to gather plants for food.

The hunter-gatherer had a much shorter 'working day' than an early farmer. Much of his work involved waiting in the right place, which might sometimes mean lounging around exchanging tall tales with fellow hunters while waiting for a herd to move into the area. Farmers, on the other hand, toiled constantly.

The main advantages of a settled lifestyle were in terms of dealing with hard times. If the game failed to appear, the hunters went hungry. A farmer might be able to rely on stored food for a time, and was settled enough to be able to preserve some of his produce. Nomadic cultures did practise food preservation to some extent but there was a limit to what a nomadic group could carry around with them. Farming-based societies were

Above: Butchering a large animal such as a mastodon was a complex task requiring a great deal of finesse to ensure that little was wasted.

thus a little more resilient in times of shortage.

Overall, becoming a farmer was not all that attractive to hunter-gatherers. It was hard work and deprived them of their traditional freedom. It did offer advantages in terms of stability and the aptitude to build larger communities, which in turn progressed technologically. However, the lack of this technology in no way suggests that hunter cultures were 'backward' or lacking in intellect. Their people were smart and tough, and very skilled in the techniques they needed.

This, along with the large-scale construction of burial mounds, indicates that the Adena and Hopewell cultures were sufficiently stable and prosperous to devote considerable resources to religion. Their people clearly cared about their spiritual well-being and were able to translate that into the creation of material items.

The Adena and later Hopewell cultures were still reliant on hunting, but they also practised farming to some extent. There is evidence that plants were already being selected for their nutritional value by the time of the Santa Rosa-Swift Creek culture, beginning a trend towards the development of high-value food crops by artificial selection similar to that which occurred elsewhere in the world.

The Adena culture disappeared around 1800 years ago; the Hopewell culture lasted another 500 years. It is not known why it disappeared, although social changes may have been responsible. As the Hopewell culture was fading a new social order arose, now known as the Mississippian culture. This was characterized by increased reliance on agriculture and the creation of permanent settlements. A complex and hierarchical social order existed, representing a major evolution of society from loose bands of hunter-gatherers into tribal states.

Meanwhile, in the southwest, farming had become common, with the Hohokam culture known to have built canals to irrigate its fields. It is possible that agriculture was introduced or copied from the people of Mexico and Central America, with whom the Hohokam culture had extensive contact. Arising at around the same time about 2000 years ago, the Mogollon culture of New Mexico did not rely on irrigation and had different farming methods to the Hohokam people.

The Anasazi people began farming maize around 1600 years ago, and gradually began to concentrate into larger urban areas.

> "...people clearly cared about their spiritual well-being and were able to translate that into the creation of material items."

Modern Native American nations of the southwestern region such as the Hopi are generally believed to be derived from the Anasazi.

THE EUROPEANS ARRIVE
Discounting the brief and ill-fated colonization attempt by Norsemen around 1000 AD, Native American society developed more or less in isolation until around 500 years ago. There was contact with Central American and Caribbean cultures of course, and Europeans probably interacted with Native Americans well before Columbus 'discovered' the continent.

Fishermen from Europe – notably Spain, Portugal and England – are known to have been active on the Grand Banks and off the coast of the North American continent by 1500, and more than likely had

Right: The arrival of Europeans in the New World ushered in five centuries of intermittent conflict. The 'Indian Wars' ended in 1890, five centuries after Columbus planted his flag.

been fishing there for some years previously. It is entirely possible that these fishermen came ashore to replenish their supplies or were forced to do so by bad weather, and encountered the local population at that time. It has been suggested that European diseases were already present in the American population when the first explorers arrived, and that lacking any immunity the casualties were limited only by the small scale of contact.

The commonly accepted date of discovery of the 'New World' is 1492, when Christopher Columbus' voyage led him to the large islands of the Caribbean. By 1500, mapping of the coast of mainland America had begun. These early expeditions may well have made contact with local populations, but there was no real need for conflict.

It was only when Europeans began to colonize their 'New World' and to plunder its riches on a large scale that they encountered the Native American in his guise as a warrior. Ultimately, the technology of the Europeans came to dominate the continent, despite the skill and prowess of the native warriors. Just as the city-builders of the Middle East ultimately defeated and drove off their nomadic neighbours, so the technologically advanced nations of Europe ultimately defeated the Native American. They did not, however, have it all their own way.

East Coast Tribes

The Eastern Seaboard region of the North American continent consists of a broad coastal plain with numerous rivers, some of which flow into very large bays. The land rises to the west, with the Atlantic Seaboard Fall Line forming the boundary of the plain. Inland, the Appalachian Mountains create a divide separating the coastal region from the interior of the continent.

While parties of Europeans may have explored deep into the North American continent, settlement was along the coast with no real attempt to colonize the far side of the Appalachian Mountains for over a century. Thus virtually all early interactions were with the Native American tribes of the coastal region.

It is not clear when Native Americans first entered the Atlantic coastal region; in all likelihood colonization began on a small scale as soon as the ice sheets retreated sufficiently to permit it. This land was characterized by extensive woodlands, which shaped the culture of the people who settled there. The woodlands provided lumber for construction as well as game for hunting and a variety of useful plant products.

The people of the northeastern woodlands developed a tribal system that may have had its origins in the Hopewell culture. The latter declined after 500 CE for reasons that remain largely unclear. Climatic or cultural changes (or both) may have contributed to the downfall of the Hopewell tradition. The succeeding Mississippian culture had a similar social structure, which was more stratified than early hunter-gatherer groupings.

The Mississippian culture was characterized by increased use of agriculture and by the adoption of the bow as the primary hunting weapon rather than the spear. This may have been a factor in the

Left: By the time this photograph was taken in the early 1900s, the Iroquois were long past the heyday of their power and had been exposed to generations of European influence.

SNYDERS

Above: Stone arrowheads and blades of the Snyders type found at the Cahokia Mounds site. Similar tools were used throughout the Mississippian culture and beyond.

Facing page: The Mississippian culture used copper for ceremonial and decorative items, such as this portrait of a warrior's face dating from around 1000 CE.

eclipse of the Hopewell culture; the greater efficiency of the bow, coupled with a need to feed an expanding population, may have contributed to over-hunting and subsequent scarcity of game. Whether or not this was the case, the hunter of the time was a bowman capable of taking quite large game on his own rather than as part of a spear-throwing team.

THE MISSISSIPPIAN AND WOODLANDS CULTURE

The Mississippian culture survived until the coming of Europeans to the continent, although it evolved over time. The tribes of the northeast woodlands on the far side of the Appalachians lived in broadly similar terrain and had contact with the Mississippian tribes, resulting in a generally similar way of life.

The tribes of the Mississippian era were typically semi-nomadic, building permanent settlements and farming the land but often leaving their homes to embark on long hunting trips. Agricultural surpluses permitted large population concentrations and the creation of great works such as the mound complex at Cahokia in modern-day Illinois. Archaeologists discovered a copper workshop at this site.

Copper had been used for tool-making and other purposes for many years before the creation of the Cahokia site. There is evidence of trade in raw copper and items made from it going back to before the rise of the Mississippian culture. Early coppersmithing was accomplished without heating the metal; instead, lumps of copper were beaten into shape. However, by the midpoint of the Mississippian culture – and possibly before it – coppersmiths were working metal in much the same way that Europeans had done.

Although worked metal was available, most of the tools used by Native Americans of the Mississippian period (around 500 AD to the arrival of European colonists) were made of traditional materials such as wood and bone. Copper remained an important ceremonial item even after tools made from more durable metals became available.

The Mississippian culture declined in the late 1300s onward. The site at Cahokia was largely abandoned and the population relocated into smaller groups. It is not clear what caused this social upheaval: the appearance of defensive structures suggests that conflict occurred, but it is not clear whether this was cause or symptom.

It is possible that the ending of the Medieval Warm Period (around 950–1250 CE) and the 'Little Ice Age' that followed disrupted the food production of the Mississippian culture and similar groups in the northeastern woodlands. Although this caused some upheaval, the overall social system remained intact.

The Native Americans of the late pre-Columbian period (i.e. the period before contact with Europeans, symbolized by the 'discovery' of the Americas by Christopher Columbus) had a stratified tribal society. The chiefs and leaders of a tribe governed their own people, but the tribe was usually part of a larger confederation. Of the confederations that existed at the time Europeans arrived on the North American continent, the best-organized was the Iroquois Confederacy.

EUROPEAN INTERLOPERS
Once European explorers had found the Americas, colonists inevitably followed. Their reasons varied; some sought the freedom to practise their chosen religion away from the endless cycles of wars, persecutions and suppressions common in Europe. Others came looking for riches: gold and silver, sugar and furs. Some sought opportunity in a new home or carved out a settlement for the sake of national pride.

Below: During the Medieval Warm Period, the Mississippian culture built large settlements and undertook ambitious building projects, notably the Cahokia site.

Europeans tended to settle where their explorers had first arrived. The Spanish initially explored the Caribbean islands and coasts, and settled there, before creating further colonies in South America. The Portuguese mostly colonized what is now Brazil, while the French had interests in both North and South America, as well as the Caribbean. English settlers landed in North America along the east coast. Most early colonies took advantage of a natural harbour or settled alongside navigable rivers, and expansion initially followed the rivers as well.

Not all of these colonies survived. Attempts by some powers to settle certain regions, such as the Portuguese in Canada, were not successful. Food shortages, bad planning and disease could cripple a colony, or the area might turn out to be economically unviable either due to difficulties in resource extraction or transportation.

Politics also played a part – colonies became bargaining chips in the affairs of the European powers, with a settlement in which a sugar island changed hands being preferable to many other concessions that might be demanded after a war. Even in times of relative peace there was some conflict, ranging from piracy and privateering to local disputes between colonists that might have nothing to do with the wider political situation.

Conflict with the Native American population was inevitable, although often not intentional. Not only did the Europeans find themselves fighting the indigenous people, they also became involved in one another's disputes and conflicts. Local warriors fought on both sides of European colonial wars, and occasionally the colonists were dragged into a conflict between indigenous tribes.

Above: The word 'Crotoan' carved by the colonists of Roanoke may have indicated that they relocated to Crotoan island, but no search was conducted.

Left: The colonization of America was a struggle for the Pilgrim Fathers from the moment they landed, and would have failed utterly but for the assistance of local tribes.

The arrival of European colonists was probably not that much of a surprise to the native population of the east coast. Explorers had been active in the region for some time, and there was probably intermittent contact with fishermen. Colonization was initially on a small scale and did not greatly worry the Native American population, who in many cases welcomed and sometimes rescued the newcomers.

The first British attempt at Roanoke Island was a complete disaster. Although reports from the colony told of great success, it seems that the reality was rather different. Short of food and lacking support from England due to conflict with Spain, the colonists were left to their own devices for years and when a new expedition reached the island there was no sign of them. Conflict with the local population was considered a likely cause, although there was no indication of fighting. It is entirely possible that the colonists simply starved or tried to relocate themselves.

The first successful colonization attempt by the British was at James Fort (later Jamestown) in Virginia. Landing in 1607, the new colonists found themselves within the territory of the Powhatan Confederacy. Wracked by disease and starvation, the Jamestown colonists survived largely due to the assistance of the Paspahegh tribe, but rapidly came into conflict with them.

Facing page: Powhatan Native Americans making a dugout canoe. Line engraving, 1590, by Theodor de Bry after John White.

Similarly, the Pilgrims of the *Mayflower* expedition, arriving in 1620, suffered from disease and shortage of food. It is notable that they brought several cannons with them, although whether the local population or other Europeans were considered the most likely threat is unclear. After struggling through a difficult first winter, the new colonists were contacted by the local population.

Both groups had been aware of one another for some time; warriors had observed the colonists' struggles to establish a settlement and the newcomers were understandably nervous. They were weakened by starvation and disease, and vastly outnumbered in a strange land. The nature of the first real contact, however, was friendly and almost casual.

"After struggling through a difficult first winter, the new colonists were contacted by the local population."

Contact was made by a member of the Abenaki tribe who had learned English from trappers and fishermen operating in what is now Maine. He had visited Europe and knew that the colonists were English. Once relations were established, the local population gave the colonists gifts of food and – more importantly in the long term – taught them how to work the land they had settled. Despite this, the colonists were

on the brink of starvation. An expedition to resupply the colony was scattered, eventually arriving after adventures in Bermuda. The situation was so bad that the colonists decided to abandon Jamestown, but encountered another fleet carrying supplies and returned to their new homes.

The colonists gradually became part of the American political landscape. There was initially no clear-cut 'us and them' where native and settler groups were concerned. The settlers entered into alliances and conflicts with some Native American tribes, assisted by or assisting others. Complex inter-tribal politics and lack of understanding of one another's culture led to misunderstandings, with the wrong tribe or colony sometimes blamed for an incident. As the settlers expanded and claimed more land, their numbers grew. Occasional skirmishes expanded into what could only be termed open warfare.

THE POWHATAN CONFEDERACY

The Powhatan Confederacy was led by the Powhatan tribe, with about 30 other tribes linked by a common language and culture. The confederacy was part of a cultural group known to modern historians as Algonquian after its common language family. Algonquian and its predecessor, known as proto-Algonquian, have been spoken in the northeastern region for at least 2500 years.

The Powhatan typically built their villages alongside rivers, constructing longhouses with a light wooden frame covered

The manner of makinge their boates. XII.

T · B ·   J2

He manner of makinge their boates in Virginia is verye wonderfull. For wheras they want Inſtruments of yron , or other like vnto ours , yet they knowe howe to make them as handſomelye , to ſaile with whear they liſte in their Riuers , and to fiſhe with all , as ours. Firſt they chooſe ſome longe , and thicke tree , accordinge to the bignes of the boate which they would frame , and make a fyre on the grownd abowt the Roote therof, kindlinge the ſame by little , and little with drie moſſe of trees , and chipps of woode that the flame ſhould not mounte opp to highe , and burne to muche of the lengte of the tree· When yt is almoſt burnt thorough, and readye to fall they make a new fyre, which they ſuffer to burne vntill the tree fall of yt owne accord. Then burninge of the topp , and bowghs of the tree in ſuche wyſe that the bodie of theſame may Retayne his iuſt lengthe , they raiſe yt vppon potes laid ouer croſſwiſe vppon forked poſts, at ſuche a reaſonable heighte as rhey may handſomlye worke vp-pó yt. Then take they of the barke with certayne ſhells: thy reſerue the,innermoſt parte of the lennke , for the nethermoſt parte of the boate. On the other ſide they make a fyre according to the lengthe of the bodye of the tree , ſauinge at both the endes. That which they thinke is ſufficientlye burned they quenche and ſcrape away with ſhells,and makinge a new fyre they burne yt agayne,and ſoe they continne ſomtymes burninge and ſometymes ſcrapinge , vntill the boate haue ſufficient bothowmes. This god indueth thiſe ſauage people with ſufficient reaſon to make thinges neceſſarie to ſerue their turnes.

in bark. They farmed the land, notably cultivating maize, beans and tobacco, and fished from canoes. These were of a dugout type, constructed by hollowing out a large log. While women stayed close to home, tending the crops and the settlement, men hunted for meat and gathered additional food items such as nuts, fruit, shellfish and root vegetables. The hunt also clothed the Powhatan, with deer hide (buckskin) favoured for moccasins and other clothing. Furs were used to make cloaks, although important individuals might instead wear a cloak of feathers.

The weapons of the Powhatan were similar to those of other tribes. Bows were the primary hunting tools, with knives, tomahawks and spears used when necessary. In war, the skills of the hunt were put to use against human targets. The Powhatan lived in a land of dense forest, through which they moved with the speed and stealth of experienced hunters. The raid and the ambush were standard tactics, with war parties striking fast then melting away if the odds turned against them.

The chief of the Powhatan Confederacy at the time of the European colonists' arrival was Wahunsenacawh, often known simply as Powhatan. His father bequeathed to him a confederation of six tribes; by 1607 he had increased this number five-fold. An astute ruler, Powhatan hoped to contain the settlers without conflict, preferring to trade with them rather than fighting.

Powhatan tried to maintain friendly relations and perhaps even co-opt the settlers under his control. Incidents of violence did occur, and Powhatan was quite willing to use raids as part of a carrot-and-stick policy. Between outbreaks of conflict he negotiated with the settlers, trading European-made tools for food. The Virginia Company, sponsor of the Jamestown colony, attempted to gain control over Powhatan and his people by presenting him with a

Facing page: Chief Wahunsenacawh, better known as Powhatan, for the tribal confederacy he ruled, was an adept politician who sought to control the European colonists.

> "The Powhatan lived in a land of dense forest, through which they moved with the speed and stealth of experienced hunters."

crown, recognizing him as king over his people and thereby by inference beholden to the English throne.

Powhatan accepted the gift but did not become a biddable colonial ruler. He did continue to foster good relations with the colonists, allowing his daughter Matoaka to marry John Rolfe, a leader among the settlers. Their relationship did not start out particularly friendly; Matoaka was taken hostage by the colonists with the intent of exchanging her for some of their people who had been captured.

Powhatan almost certainly viewed the marriage as a useful political gambit, and a state of more-or-less peace continued for some time. Matoaka – better known by her mildly insulting nickname Pocahontas ('spoiled child' or 'naughty one') – accompanied her husband to England on a tour intended to garner support for the colony. She died of an illness, possibly smallpox, while she was there.

The legend that Matoaka saved the life of the English settler John Smith when he was captured by the Powhatan was a self-serving invention. Far from being on the brink of execution, Smith was treated honourably by the Powhatan and was not in need of rescue by Matoaka, who at that time would have been a child. It is unlikely that the powerful and sometimes harsh chief of the Powhatan Confederacy that bore his name would be turned aside from his chosen course of action in this manner. Certainly there was no romance between Smith and his alleged saviour. When Matoaka encountered him in London she is said to have publicly snubbed him, and his claims about her coming to his rescue only began several years after the incident. His reports of the time do not mention it.

The mostly fictional story of Pocahontas has contributed to popular misconceptions about the early contact between settlers and Native Americans. The situation was complex, with all parties having their own needs and agendas. Some decisions were made for bad reasons – perhaps greed, a desire for the excitement of conflict or a chance to demonstrate prowess in combat or contempt for another group's way of life. Most were motivated by perceived necessity or political advantage. Indeed, the situation in North America in the early

Below: Matoaka, daughter of Chief Powhatan, was baptized and took the name Rebecca before her marriage to John Rolfe, but is better known by her derogatory nickname of Pocahontas.

1600s fits the old adage of only
being simple if you pick a side. It
can most fairly be described as a
complex interaction between many
factors, coloured in the grey of
politics rather than simple black
and white.

Chief Powhatan attempted to
gain control over the Jamestown
settlers by cutting off trade, since
he knew they were dependent on
his people to supplement their
own efforts to produce food. This
resulted in what became known
as the 'starving time' and the
temporary abandonment of the
colony. However, the colonists
were resupplied and continued
to expand. They allowed their
livestock to wander through
cultivated areas, causing significant
destruction. This may not have
been intentional, but since the
Native Americans practised a just-
enough style of food production
the effects were significant.

The cycle of conflict and relative
peace continued until the death
of Powhatan in 1618, with the
period 1609–1614 known as the
First Powhatan War. By this time
the colony at Jamestown had been
expanded and was developing
an economy based upon tobacco
production. Powhatan's brother
Opechancanough decided to rid
himself of the colonists, bringing
about a series of wars. Hostilities
opened with a surprise attack on
the colonists, which killed about
a quarter of their 1200 or so
population.

The cannon had proven decisive
in earlier clashes. An attack on the
initial camp in 1607 was broken up
by cannon fire from the explorers'
ships, and the selection of the
settlement site had been partially
governed by the availability of a hill
upon which to mount an artillery
platform. Once more the colonists
were able to drive off the attack,
and when news reached England
the reaction had far-reaching

Above: An old and sick man when he was captured by the English, Chief Opechancanough rebuked his captors that he would have treated their leaders better had the situation been reversed.

consequences. Ultimately the Virginia Company was dissolved and Jamestown became a royal colony. Rather than a militia formed from people engaged in a private endeavour, the Powhatan were now in conflict with the throne of England.

The Second Powhatan War (1622–32), initially in the form of raids in force to disrupt native food production. Nomadic hunter-gatherers could have relocated or hunted elsewhere, but the Powhatan were a settled people dependent largely upon agriculture. Attempts to make peace collapsed in treachery, with the colonists attacking the peace delegation in revenge for

the casualties inflicted in the original attack.

The Second Powhatan War came to an end in 1632, with the Powhatan driven from much of their land. They launched a new offensive in 1644, initially meeting with success. Despite inflicting heavy casualties, the Powhatan were unable to drive the colonists off and lost more territory to counter-offensives. These gains were secured by the construction of forts.

The Virginia colonists are known to have obtained slaves in the early days of the colony, but may have initially treated them as indentured workers who would be freed eventually. By 1640, however, slavery was practised in the colony, and Native American captives were sold as slaves. Captured in 1645, Opechancanough himself did not meet this fate but was murdered by his captors. His successor, Necotowance, agreed a treaty the following year.

The Powhatan Wars set the tone for future interactions and conflicts between settlers and Native Americans. Bad blood was engendered by surprise attacks and massacres, and the mistrust and hatred that many colonists felt was transferred to other native groupings. The newcomers were at times unaware – or simply did not care – that they were dealing with different tribes or even entire confederations. However, this did not create an entirely 'us and them' situation – both settlers and native confederations were willing to use the other in their struggles against their rivals.

THE PEQUOT WAR

The Pequot were among the first tribes encountered by the European settlers, living along the valley of the Thames in modern Connecticut. They were allied with the Mohegan, who rebelled in 1632 against what they saw as an unequal partnership. The leader of this rebellion was Uncas, who believed he should lead the allied tribes. His rebellion failed, but over time he fostered relations with the English settlers of the area in the hope of obtaining their support.

Relations between the Pequot and the newcomers were initially friendly, but encroachment by the settlers into Pequot territory resulted in increasing tensions. A series of violent incidents occurred, with kidnappings and murders prompting retaliation in kind or destructive raids on villages and settlements.

Below: A contemporary diagram of the attack on the Pequot stronghold on the Mystic River, showing colonial musketeers and their allies from the Mohegan tribe.

The focus of the Pequot campaign was Fort Saybrook, a fortified settlement constructed in 1635–36. It essentially became besieged, although not quite in the sense of European warfare. Instead, the Pequot maintained skirmishing parties near the settlement and attacked anyone who came out or tried to reach the fort. The defenders responded with cannon fire and their own sorties, resulting in months of small-scale skirmishing during which both sides learned much about the other's way of fighting.

As Pequot raids on other settlements increased in severity, the settlers raised a militia and launched a punitive expedition. The intent was to destroy the Pequot's crops and nearby settlements. In this, they were assisted by warriors of the Narragansett tribe and the Mohegan, although the situation might best be described as 'the enemy of my enemy is the enemy of my enemy… and quite probably nothing more.'

The expedition that set out in May 1637 serves as an example of the politics of the time. The Narragansett and Mohegan may well have considered themselves fortunate to have found some foreigners willing to fight their enemies, essentially using the English militia as mercenaries; the English thought they had recruited some useful guides and additional skirmishers for their own campaign.

The Pequot stronghold at Mystic River was attacked by this joint force, part of which managed to get inside its palisade. There, the attackers were outmatched and set fire to the village while trying to fight their way out. The conflagration that followed killed hundreds of Pequot people, and those who managed to escape were attacked once they were outside the defences.

Retiring after the massacre at Mystic River, the expedition came under repeated attack from warriors who had arrived too late to defend the stronghold. These attacks were beaten off with heavy losses, with the overall result that Pequot power was broken and the survivors attempted to leave the area. Few succeeded. The tribe essentially ceased to exist, with its remaining people absorbed into other tribes.

The Mohegan and Narragansett warriors who had witnessed the assault on Mystic River found the savagery of the Europeans' warmaking distasteful, but thought it necessary to maintain their alliance. An uneasy peace began in 1637 with the ending

> ## "The Mohegan and Narragansett warriors who had witness the assault on Mystic River found the savagery of the Europeans war making distasteful."

of the Pequot War, and although there was small-scale conflict here and there the Connecticut region did not see a major clash between settlers and Native Americans for almost four decades.

THE IROQUOIS CONFEDERACY

The Iroquois Confederacy was composed originally of five tribes, later six. These five, the Seneca,

Facing page: A French engraving dating from 1664, showing the daily life of an Iroquois village. The open-ended longhouse would have been home to several families.

Wampum

Above: The ceremonial giving of wampum belts like this Shawnee example was a mark of respect and an important part of resolving issues between tribes.

Wampum is a form of cylindrical bead made from the shells of the channelled whelk. It was used to make belts that had various ceremonial functions, notably establishing a person's credentials or trustworthiness. Legend has it that the Great Peacemaker of the Iroquois people used wampum to encode messages. The giving of a wampum belt marked an important event or recognition of an individual's achievements.

Wampum was used among the Iroquois as a badge of office for chiefs and clan mothers, and as a means by which messengers could establish that they were carrying valid information. It became an important trade item and, inevitably perhaps, factories were set up to mass-produce wampum for trade. This reduced its economic value, but socially it remained an important item.

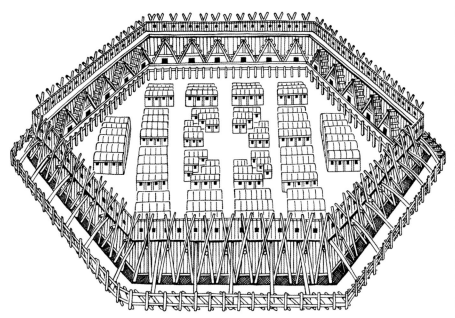

Above: The Iroquois well understood the value of fortification, building wooden palisades to protect their villages from raiders.

Facing page: At the Battle of Long Sault in 1660, Iroquois warriors improvised wooden mantlets to cover their advance against the muskets of the French defenders.

Cayuga, Onondaga, Oneida and Mohawk, were linguistically related to one another but not to the surrounding tribes, suggesting that they were relatively new arrivals in the northeastern woodlands. It is possible that the Iroquois were related to the Cherokee, with whom they shared some linguistic similarities.

Although probably of distant origins, the Iroquois had a similar way of life to their neighbours. They dwelled in similar bark-covered longhouses, and indeed referred to themselves as 'people of the longhouse' (Haudenosaunee). A single longhouse might be home to as many as 20 families, with men moving in with their new wives when they married.

Society was matrilineal, with clan membership based upon descent through female ancestors and multiple clans forming a tribe. The elder women of the tribes wielded great power, and although the chief was male he was selected by the female elders and the ceremonial items denoting

his status were the property of the elders, not the chief.

Europeans first started settling the Iroquois home region in what is now New York state, although their power increased over time and they came to dominate a much wider area. The Iroquois Confederacy (or Iroquois League as it was also called) was founded by a man known as the Peacemaker, who demonstrated the strength of a unit by tying together a bundle of arrows. One could be broken easily; together they could not. This concept was similar to that espoused by some European societies, notably the Roman Empire, but the confederacy was formed long before European contact and thus the idea must have developed independently.

The Peacemaker set out the laws and customs that governed the confederacy and its member tribes. Known as the Great Law of Peace, it created a democratic system whereby the confederacy was governed by 50 men known as Hoyaneh or Sachems, who formed a grand council that made laws and passed judgements by consensus. As with tribal chiefs, Hoyaneh were male but they were selected and could be removed from office by the clan mothers.

Although governed by a Great Law of Peace, the Iroquois were formidable warriors. This was out of necessity, as they had potential enemies all around them. Before the Peacemaker built their alliance, they fought one another. Once the confederation was established, warfare against neighbouring tribes was common. The threat of attack was sufficiently great that the

Native American Strategy

Above: Raids not only inflicted casualties and damaged the settlers' economy; they caused the settlers to fear that a raiding party lurked behind every tree.

Native American strategy was not concerned with terrain objectives; once an enemy was defeated or driven off his land it could be used, but there was no need to take and hold ground. Likewise, other than defending a settlement there was no need to fight if the odds were not good. Instead, the Native American warrior raided and ambushed his enemies, fighting on his own terms.

Native American strategy was built around weakening the enemy's will to fight and his economic capabilities. Both were achieved through raiding. Direct attacks on strong places such as the forts set up by Europeans or fortified settlements were costly and not always effective. Such assaults were made at times, but the Native Americans preferred to make the surrounding countryside highly dangerous and essentially besiege them in their forts.

Fights with enemy war parties were an acceptable tactic providing there was something to gain, but for the most part attacks were made on relatively soft targets such as small settlements. Raids on isolated farms that had no military significance were not made out of spite, although on some occasions they were conducted with vengeance in mind. The intent was to make the region untenable for enemies and to reduce their ability to feed themselves. Captured women and children were typically absorbed into the tribe while men were killed, often through torture.

The fear this engendered not only helped induce the enemy to give up the fight, but made people fearful to go out hunting or even work the land. The Europeans might be well protected in their forts but if they could not make money from furs, or even harvest their crops, then there was no point in their remaining in the New World. The Native Americans did not need to defeat the newcomers in the field unless their own settlements were threatened. All they had to do was make their land untenable.

This strategy was not really any different from that used against other tribes, and represents a slightly different emphasis on territorial control to that favoured by Europeans. Rather than capturing ground, the Native American approach was more about exerting influence. It did not matter whose flag was planted in a piece of ground; what was important was who could operate there.

Iroquois fortified their villages with a wooden palisade. The settlement housed anything from a few hundred to 3000 people and was semi-permanent. Every 30 years or so the village was relocated as natural resources such as bark became depleted and the land less fertile.

The arrival of Europeans upset the local balance of power. The Huron and Mohican tribes obtained firearms in trade and used them against the Iroquois. This disadvantage was offset by the military capabilities of the highly stable Iroquois Confederacy. Although the member tribes did not always get along, they had a system in place for the resolution of disputes and an incentive to use it. This permitted the confederacy to turn its strength outward to a degree unmatched by other tribal groups.

THE BEAVER WARS

From 1642 to 1698, a series of conflicts took place that established the Iroquois as the dominant power in the north-eastern woodland region. Known collectively as the Beaver Wars, this period brought the Iroquois into conflict with French settlers as well as several other native tribes.

The French had initially established a fishing presence on the Grand Banks, then moved inland in search of furs. They made an alliance with the local tribes and generally got along well with them, supplying weapons in exchange for furs. This increased pressure on the Iroquois, who were concerned at the growing power of their enemies and wanted to control the fur trade.

European traders were keen to obtain beaver pelts in particular, and were willing to trade firearms

Above: Attacks on settlements such as that at Lachine in Canada in August 1689 were characterized by massacre and destruction. The Iroquois were not interested in conquest; only the defeat of their enemies.

and tools for them. These in turn permitted more efficient hunting, which depleted the local beaver population. The Iroquois made war upon their enemies, such as the Huron, in order to gain access to their hunting grounds and to set themselves up in a position where European trade went through their territory.

The conflict began with Iroquois attacks on Huron villages, driving the Huron northward by 1649. The French then began trading with the Ottawa, leading to escalation and widening of the conflict. Raids against French settlements began and went on for some years without a decisive result. At the same time, the Iroquois were pushing westward towards the Great Lakes and the Mississippi, displacing some tribes and absorbing others. Some of these, such as the Lakota, moved onto the Great Plains, forcing a major change in their way of life. Others tried to find new territory, often causing secondary conflicts with the tribes they encountered.

The French reaction was to deploy regular troops and make punitive expeditions into Iroquois territory. Although the Iroquois were able to avoid defeat by skirmishing and withdrawing in the face of large organized forces, they could not prevent the destruction of their homes and crops. Food shortages eventually forced the Iroquois to negotiate a peace treaty, which lasted for several years. In the meantime, some of the French soldiers were withdrawn and a militia system was set up in the French colonies. The peace collapsed in 1683,

again with control of the fur trade as the central issue. Both sides attacked one another's settlements for a time, but the changing political situation forced the French to seek a peaceful end to the conflict. Their real enemies in the New World were the English, and the constant cycle of raid and counter-raid only depleted their strength. In 1701, a treaty between Native American tribes, English

> *"At the same time, the Iroquois were pushing westward towards the Great Lakes and the Mississippi, displacing some tribes and absorbing others."*

and French settlers was signed. Under its terms, the Iroquois allowed some of the displaced tribes to return to their lands.

In 1722, the five nations of the Iroquois were joined by a sixth. The Tuscarora people, originally of North Carolina, were pushed northward by English expansion in the area and eventually joined the Iroquois Confederacy. Some documents refer to the confederacy as the 'five nations' before 1722 and the 'six nations' thereafter.

KING PHILIP'S WAR

Shortly after relations were established with the English colonists, they were approached by Massasoit, a chief of the Wampanoag people. Massasoit established good relations with the newcomers and fostered trade. He was able to maintain peace despite increasing encroachment by the expanding colonies, but by the time he was succeeded by his son Wamsutta tensions had reached an unacceptable level.

Wamsutta had little chance to take control of the situation; he died in 1662 just a year after his father. Leadership of the tribe passed to Metacom (sometimes called Metacomet), who was known to the English as Philip of Pokanoket or King Philip. The colonists traded firearms among other goods to the Native American tribes in exchange for land, and then demanded the guns be returned in order to keep the peace.

For over a decade, Metacom was successful in his dealings with the colonists, ensuring they did not push too far in negotiations by keeping them concerned about the outbreak of war. Eventually, in 1675 war did indeed begin. The trigger incident was the execution in Plymouth of three Native Americans for murder, but the situation was such that conflict was inevitable sooner or later. The resulting conflict became known as King Philip's War. It pitted a confederation of tribes – the Abenaki, Mohawk, Narragansett and Nipmuc, as well as Metacom's own Wampanoag – against the colonists. The first year saw about 3000 casualties inflicted upon the Europeans in exchange for around 600 native warriors.

Firearms of the Early 1600s

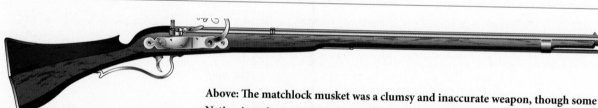

Above: The matchlock musket was a clumsy and inaccurate weapon, though some Native American warriors were skilled enough to hunt beaver with it.

The first explorers and colonists into the New World were armed with smoothbore matchlock weapons that were neither accurate nor easy to carry. Such weapons were primarily useful in a defensive action, firing from behind a rampart, or in massed formations shooting at a large target such as another formed unit. They lacked the accuracy, precision and responsiveness required for sharpshooting in the North American forest.

These were the guns used against and by Native American warriors in the early 1600s, and although they were supplanted by much better flintlock weapons from the 1650s or so, they continued to be used in many areas. This was partly due to the expense and difficulty in obtaining newer weapons, and partly because those who could get the new generation of firearms were likely to offset the cost by selling their old guns to anyone willing to pay for them.

The matchlock relied, as the name suggests, on a slow-match brought into contact with the powder charge. Ignition of the powder was not instant and often failed to occur at all. This, along with the weight and general awkwardness of the weapon, made it virtually impossible to hit a moving target.

A Native American warrior armed with a bow had numerous advantages over the matchlock-armed European, at least in the open. He could change position more quickly and shoot more rapidly – and with greater range and accuracy – and had at least a reasonable chance of hitting a fleeting target. It was not until the development of improved firearms that the advantage shifted.

Native American Tactics: The Battle of Braddock's Field

In July 1755, a force of English regulars under General Braddock, for whom the subsequent action was named, advanced on the French Fort Duquesne in what is now Pennsylvania. His expedition was reinforced by local militia and a young colonel of militia by the name of George Washington. Opposing this force was a mix of French troops, militia raised in what is now Canada and native allies.

The English regulars were disciplined and steady but were not used to warfare in the Americas, having recently come from Ireland. They lacked local scouts, since General Braddock did not see the need to recruit them. He advanced rapidly with a flying column, with reinforcements following with cannons and supply wagons.

The French attempted to intercept Braddock's advance and set up an ambush, but were confounded by his use of the flying column, resulting in an encounter battle. Although outnumbered, the French/Native American force had the advantage of knowing the terrain, shooting from among the trees and shifting position to make their numbers seem greater. The English tried to make use of formations better suited to set-piece battles in Europe, and succeeded mainly in making themselves better targets for skirmishers. When some of the settler militia dispersed into positions of cover, they were fired upon by the regulars in the mistaken belief they were the enemy.

Despite holding firm for about three hours, the English regulars began to retire when Braddock was mortally wounded. They owed their escape to two factors: the leadership of George Washington and the rearguard action fought by the Virginia militia, who used the same tactics as their enemies.

Falling back on the supporting force, Braddock's flying column was able to escape the disaster, although numerous cannon and quantities of supplies were destroyed to prevent them falling into enemy hands. The action was one of many that demonstrated that effective warfare in the Americas required the adoption of tactics used by those who lived there. This lesson was not lost on George Washington, who put it to use some years later during the American Revolution.

Below: Although the English would try to repeat the tactics of Braddock's Field in the War of Independence, George Washington learned a valuable lesson there about warfare in the Americas.

Although successful at first, Metacom's coalition was defeated by logistics as much as anything else. As it became increasingly difficult to feed his forces they deserted, leaving Metacom much weakened. He retreated to Mount Hope but was found by his enemies and captured. The war ended with the beheading of Metacom. Such fear did he inspire in the colonists that his severed head was displayed at Plymouth for the next 25 years.

THE FRENCH AND INDIAN WAR

The French and Indian War of 1754–63 was fought between European powers, but it had far-reaching consequences for the Native American people and involved numerous tribes on both sides. Europeans tended to view events in the New World as an extension of the Seven Years War (1756–63), which resulted from territorial losses in earlier conflicts. Britain and France found themselves on opposite sides, with clashes occurring wherever their interests or territories were in proximity. This included India as well as the New World.

While it may well have appeared to the European commanders that they were involved in a fight for supremacy in the New World and that their local allies were merely pawns in the game, the Native American perspective was in many cases quite different. Conflict between the new arrivals was part of the local

Right: Although the Narragansett were not directly involved in King Philip's War they were attacked in December 1675, resulting in what became known as the Great Swamp Fight.

Below: Payta Kootha of the Shawnee people was a skilled hunter and well-travelled diplomat who helped resolve disputes among the villages of his people.

political situation and might be exploited for the gain of one tribe or another, or might be viewed as an upheaval not dissimilar to a drought or a particularly stormy season – something to be survived and overcome. The war was not a simple matter with two sides; there

> *"...the Wabanaki Confederacy established a buffer zone of colonist settlements..."*

were many factions with a complex web of alliances, old feuds and hopes for the outcome.

The French found allies among the people of the Wabanaki Confederacy, who had enjoyed good relations with the French settlers and indeed found it useful

to allow them to settle certain lands. In so doing, the Wabanaki Confederacy established a buffer zone of colonist settlements – with cannon and the support of troops from the homeland if seriously threatened – between themselves and tribes with whom they had a history of conflict. Other allies of the French included the Shawnee.

At the time of European expansion into the Americas, the Shawnee held extensive territories in the region of the Ohio River. Their semi-nomadic society was based upon agriculture, primarily maize cultivation, and was probably derived from the Hopewell culture. In the period up to 1700 or so, the Shawnee built mound structures and also used those of preceding societies such as the Fort Ancient site. These mound complexes were ceremonial rather than defensive sites.

Below: The dugout canoe and the wigwam were characteristic of the tribes of the northeastern woodlands, making sophisticated use of naturally occurring resources.

The dwellings of the Shawnee were rounded structures usually known as wigwams, or wikkums in the northeastern region and wikiup in more western areas. Construction used poles formed from saplings and bent inward to create a dome, over which an outer covering of bark or other materials such as hides was applied. Because it was the first such structure to be encountered by Europeans, there is a tendency to apply the term 'wigwam' to any vaguely similar dwelling made by Native Americans.

Clothing was similar to that of other tribes living in the same area, although after Europeans arrived the Shawnee adopted some elements of their dress. These were sometimes but not always altered to suit their preferences, and were influenced by the French settlers and traders they encountered before other newcomers.

Relations with the French settlers were generally good, with trade to mutual benefit. However, the politics of the New World were in no way divorced from those of the Old. France and England were at odds over many matters, from territorial and economic ambition to religious differences. It was inevitable that as they expanded into the Americas these conflicts would be carried over into a new theatre of war.

English allies included the Iroquois and the Cherokee, who were linguistically related. The Cherokee are widely thought to have migrated into the eastern coastal region from the Great Lakes around 4000–5000 years ago. Like many other Native American

Above: The Cherokee built log cabins as their homes rather than the lighter shelters used by many other tribes of the region. Many European dwellings used a similar design.

Right: The attack on the surrendered garrison of Fort William Henry was portrayed as treachery on the part of bloodthirsty savages, but the real reasons remain unclear.

people they had a matriarchal society in which specialist clans existed, all working towards the good of the tribe as a whole. The Deer clan contained the best hunters, the Bird clan provided spiritual guidance and the Wolf clan were the warriors of the tribe.

The Cherokee built log cabins as dwellings rather than the lighter structures favoured by other tribes. Contact with Europeans brought a devastating disease epidemic, but afterward the Cherokee prospered in trade and would eventually adopt some elements of the Europeans' way of life. At the outbreak of the French and Indian war they were willing to fight alongside the settlers' militia. However, the English were slow to make use of their assistance.

ENGLISH SETBACKS

The English settlers were repeatedly defeated by the French in the early stages of the war. The 1755 expedition to capture Fort Duquesne from the French ended in disaster at the Battle of Braddock's Field, notably due to the fact that the French had assistance from their allies while the British commander thought he could do without them. Non-British settlers and local tribes were expelled from some areas where the British did achieve success, setting an example for future treatment of the indigenous population.

In August 1757, the French attacked Fort William Henry with the assistance of a mixed contingent of Native American warriors. Accounts exist of Native American warriors enjoying the fireworks as artillery played back and forth between the fort and the siegeworks, but with no relief coming the garrison commander agreed to surrender on generous terms.

What followed is subject to great controversy. The English

"Ironically perhaps, many tribes were inclined to support the English in their attempts to bring the colonies under control."

garrison and population were apparently permitted to march out with the honours of war, although with no ammunition for their weapons and under French escort. It remains unclear whether the subsequent attack on the garrison was sanctioned or not, or exactly why it took place, but several parties of Native American warriors attacked the surrendered English, killing many and carrying others off as captives or slaves. English accounts probably make more of the massacre than the reality, but nevertheless casualties were serious.

It may be that the warriors did not understand what was going on and thought their enemies were getting away, or the attack might have been the work of those with

a grudge or who simply wanted a fight. It may have resulted from hate, misunderstanding, escalation of the actions of a few hotheads or some combination of these factors. Whatever the truth, this incident escalated the bad blood that existed between many tribes and the settlers.

The British gradually gained the upper hand in the American theatre of war and elsewhere, eventually leading to treaties that gave the British control over Canada and the eastern part of the North American continent. This had serious implications for those tribes that had sided with or favoured the French. The colonists were also greatly affected, as the cost of the war resulted in heavy taxation that created resentment. Perceived mismanagement of the affairs of the American colonies, and the resulting conflict with Native American tribes, was another factor in the increasing disaffection felt by many colonists. This would eventually lead to the American Revolution.

THE AMERICAN REVOLUTION

Disatisfaction with England eventually caused the colonies to declare independence, which the English crown could not tolerate. Although primarily a conflict between Europeans, the revolution involved large numbers of Native Americans. Ironically perhaps, many tribes were inclined to support the English in their attempts to bring the colonies under control. This stemmed from policies intended to slow down expansion of the colonies into Native American lands.

Above: The bloody Battle of Oriskany in August 1777 pitted American loyalists and rebels, both with Native American allies, against one another.

These policies were not followed out of any great regard for the rights of the local population, but were mainly aimed at reducing threats to the fur trade and other economic activity. Wars with the local tribes were costly and could disrupt English endeavours in the New World, and were best avoided. The colonists, on the other hand, needed land and resources to build their own economy rather than feeding that of the home country and were more inclined to encroach on Native American territory.

The colonists had advantages over the English regulars sent against them, at least in the field. They had learned hard lessons in warfare against the native warriors, and now applied them against the forces of the Crown. The disciplined formations of the English were an easy target for rebel marksmen, whereas their volley fire represented overkill against individual targets if they could be discerned at all.

Of course, the English learned lessons in the War of Independence, notably the need to field light infantry and sharpshooters. Troops armed with rifles (as opposed to smoothbore muskets) began to appear, although it would be a few years before the British Army began to field regular rifle units or light infantry regiments of its own rather than using foreign troops in this role.

The English most definitely had the advantage in set-piece battles or sieges of fortified cities, but ultimately they were forced to concede defeat by a combination of American tenacity and French intervention. Neither side took much notice of the Native American tribes during the subsequent negotiations, even though native warriors had played an important part as scouts and auxiliaries.

Above: The Battle of Wyoming in July 1778 was a resounding defeat for American rebels at the hands of English forces and their Iroquois allies.

The politics of the revolution affected the native tribes as much as the colonists. The Iroquois Confederation was split, with the Mohawks siding with the English and the Oneida with the rebels. After the war, retaliation was almost indiscriminate. Tribes that had supported the rebels were attacked alongside those that had fought against the emerging United States. The Iroquois Confederation was badly damaged and never recovered from these events.

INDIAN REMOVALS

Despite the admiration of many notable figures in the American Revolution for the native way of life, and what seems to have been genuine good intentions in many parts, the new United States encroached ever more on traditional Native American lands. The solution, as seen by many, was relocation.

Some tribes agreed to be resettled, others resisted. Even those who went willingly suffered great hardship, and in many cases the conduct of those enforcing the resettlement was not honourable. Documents such as the 1787 Northwest Ordinance made provision for the protection of Native American land and rights, but over time this attitude changed. In 1830 the Indian Removal Act was passed, which supposedly provided for voluntary relocation but could be used to force tribes to move. Many tribes were beginning to be assimilated into the emerging United States, and in the longer term might have become an important part of its development. However, despite becoming known as the Five Civilized Tribes, the Cherokee, Chickasaw, Choctaw, Muskogee and Seminole were removed from their ancestral lands and granted territory west of the Mississippi.

First to be relocated were the Choctaw, despite the fact that they had sided with the colonies' attempt to gain independence. The Choctaw endured so much hardship on the way to their new homes that the march became known as a 'trail

of tears and death'. Thousands of Native Americans perished from disease, starvation, accident and hostile action. Their destination was at the time known as Indian Territory, consisting of more or less everything west of the Mississippi that was not part of Louisiana or Missouri. The territory was later reduced to allow settlers to expand across the continent, and came to roughly correspond to modern-day Oklahoma.

Among those who resisted relocation were the Seminole, who had moved into northern Florida in the mid-1700s. The Seminole were willing to take in refugees

from other tribes, escaped slaves and more or less anyone else who wanted to join them, and they had grown into a powerful tribe. They farmed the higher, dryer ground and hunted in the wetlands around their homes.

The First Seminole War (1817–18) was not fought over territory or relocation, but resulted from the efforts of the United States government to recover escaped slaves living with the Seminole. Adopted by the tribe, the runaways were defended by it. Some villages were dispersed and Spanish holdings in the area were captured by the United States.

Flintlock Firearms

Left: The flintlock pistol was a weapon for close-range personal defence rather than the battlefield, but in a close-quarters scramble amid the trees it could be a life-saver.

From the mid-1600s to the mid-1800s, the flintlock was the standard firearm mechanism. Rather than a slow-match brought into contact with powder, the flintlock used a piece of flint to strike a shower of sparks and ignite the charge. This was by no means 100 per cent reliable, but a flintlock weapon could be carried primed but uncocked, and brought quickly into action.

This made it possible to carry several pistols ready for use, which was useful for cavalry, standard-bearers or individuals who might find themselves in the thick of a fight. One or more flintlock pistols might be carried as a back-up, but it was longarms that were the decisive weapon for military use, and which were most useful in hunting.

Most flintlock longarms were smoothbore muskets, passably accurate out to 100m (330ft) or so and relatively quick to load and fire. They were still best suited to volley fire against large formations, but a skilled user – such as a hunter who

used his flintlock every day – might well be able to hit a moving target such as an enemy dashing through the trees.

Variants appeared, ranging from short bell-mouthed blunderbusses, shotguns, double- and even multi-barrelled weapons as well as rifles. The latter were slow to load since their projectile was a tight fit in the barrel, but produced a higher muzzle velocity and much greater accuracy. The long 'Pennsylvania Rifle' produced for the Continental Army was accurate out to 300m (985ft) or so, and was prized by all who could obtain one.

SEMINOLE WARS

The Second Seminole War (1835–42) broke out when the tribe refused to relinquish lands granted to them as a reservation and accept relocation west of the Mississippi. Under the leadership of Osceola, the Seminole fought an effective guerrilla war for seven years. Other tribes had been defeated when their homes were attacked, but the Seminole were willing to retreat into the everglades where their non-combatants could not be found, and to ambush anyone who came looking. The early phase of the Second Seminole War came to an end in 1837 when Osceola and other chiefs accepted an invitation to peace negotiations but were seized despite the conditions of the truce. After this the war took on a more disjointed and intermittent character, although it did not end until the majority of Seminole agreed to be relocated in 1842. The Third Seminole War (1855–58) was little more than a mopping-up operation in which remaining Seminole holdouts were located and eventually bribed into moving west. Some Seminole remained in Florida, eventually achieving Federal recognition.

By the middle of the 19th century there were few Native Americans left east of the Appalachians. Popular culture has come to associate their tribes with the great plains rather than the woodlands of the east coast, largely due to the popularity of Western movies. Some of the people driven west had to learn a new way of life, and would fight with the Federal government again as the 'European' Americans spread westwards in search of riches and land.

Below: Attacks launched by the Seminole may have been intended to draw a pursuit or punitive expedition into the everglades and eventual ambush.

The Hunter's Bow

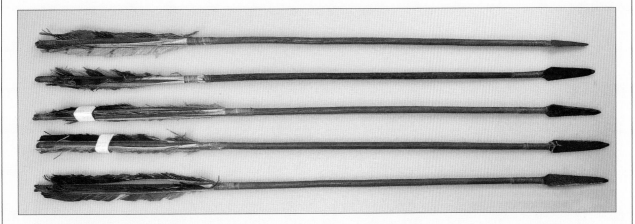

Above: With its straight grain, Osage orangewood was an ideal material for bow-making. The bow was never fully supplanted by firearms due to its unique advantages.

The bow replaced the spear as the primary weapon of the Native American hunter and warrior around 500 AD. Although it was more difficult to make, the bow offered several advantages. It had a greater range and velocity, which in turn improved accuracy and penetrating power. A hunter armed with a bow was more likely to get into shooting range than a spear-thrower, and more likely to make a kill if he did. The movement of drawing and loosing a bow was smaller, giving the prey less warning and possibly not giving away the shooter's position.

Bows had other advantages over spears and even firearms. Ammunition supply was always a concern with guns – along with noise that would scare off a whole herd as soon as the first shot was fired – whereas numerous arrowheads could be produced

from a piece of flint or the bones of a prey animal. Stone-tipped arrows were almost as lethal as metal arrowheads, which were available in some areas. Thus the bowman could keep himself supplied with arrows while the rifleman was dependent on trade for ammunition.

The bow itself was a complex item, created from a composite of materials that varied from one region to another. Bows used from horseback tended to be shorter, and other material considerations included local variations in temperature and humidity, as well of course as to what was available.

Arrows were produced using young shoots that might be heated to straighten them or shaved down to leave a straight core. The tip might be bone or flint, and after contact with Europeans other materials such as glass might be used if it was available. Tips were

generally attached by inserting the base of the arrowhead in a slit cut in the front of the arrow then tying it in place with sinew.

Although their use of bone- or stone-tipped arrows qualifies the Native Americans who defeated the Norse colonists around 1000 CE as 'Stone Age' warriors, their weapons were highly effective in skilled hands – and a hunter who lived or died by his shooting skills was likely to be very effective indeed. Similar 'Stone Age' weapon technology proved effective when native and settler populations came into conflict in the 1600s.

The bows available to the Native American warrior in the 1600s were superior in range, accuracy and rate of fire to the colonists' gunpowder weapons, and it was not until many years later that repeating firearms appeared that were truly superior to the bows of the native population.

Northern Tribes

Between the Appalachian Mountains and the Great Plains, the landscape is dominated by lakes and rivers. The Ohio and Tennessee rivers come together and ultimately flow into the Mississippi, joined by many other rivers to create an immense drainage basin that was home to several early Native American civilizations.

The Ohio River basin and the shores of the Great Lakes were home to numerous tribes before the arrival of Europeans, and others were pushed into the area by pressures along the eastern coast. European explorers penetrated into this area within a few years of landing in the Americas, but it was many decades before white settlers crossed the Appalachians in numbers and became involved in the politics of the region. Events in the Ohio basin had a profound effect upon the development of the United States and the fate of the Native American nations.

The distinction between the USA and Canada is of course a modern construct – a line on a map drawn as modern states began to emerge. A tribe described in a modern text as 'crossing into Canada' would not have thought of it that way, they were merely moving from one place to another. Although the territory of other tribes was a consideration, modern state or national borders had no meaning.

In the 1600s, terrain features were far more important than political distinctions. Terrain dictated where a tribe could hunt and live, and what resources were available to its members. Boundaries were based not necessarily on distance, but upon time. Good hunting grounds might lie close to the territory of a tribe but might not be used because it took too long to get there through difficult terrain. A river might provide mobility or be an obstacle, depending on the tribe's talent for building canoes.

Left: The Inuit remained in the far north and retained much of their pre-migration way of life. For them the Ice Age never really ended.

Settlement of what is now Canada was by way of gradual migration as the ice retreated and game moved north. Some areas were more attractive than others for tribes to settle – the St Lawrence River Valley and the Great Lakes provided fertile soil and abundant game, for example, creating ideal conditions for settlement. Further north life was harder, and the tribes that pushed up into the far north adopted a different lifestyle to those that settled around the Ohio and St Lawrence rivers.

IROQUOIS INFLUENCES

The Iroquois Confederacy was powerful in the eastern part of the Ohio Valley. Its members may have shared a common ancestry with some of the Great Lakes tribes; the proto-Iroquoian language was spoken in the Great Lakes region in the distant past and there are linguistic links to the tribes of the area. However, this did not prevent the Iroquois from declaring war on the people of the region when necessary.

Conflict had occurred sporadically during the entire history of the Iroquois, but the Beaver Wars of the 17th century resulted in large-scale warfare that ultimately drove tribes west onto the Great Plains or north into Canada. Some were effectively wiped out or absorbed by the victors. The wars began in the 1640s with a campaign against

Below: The Five Nations of the Iroquois Confederacy represented one of the most powerful political units in the New World at the time of the Europeans' arrival.

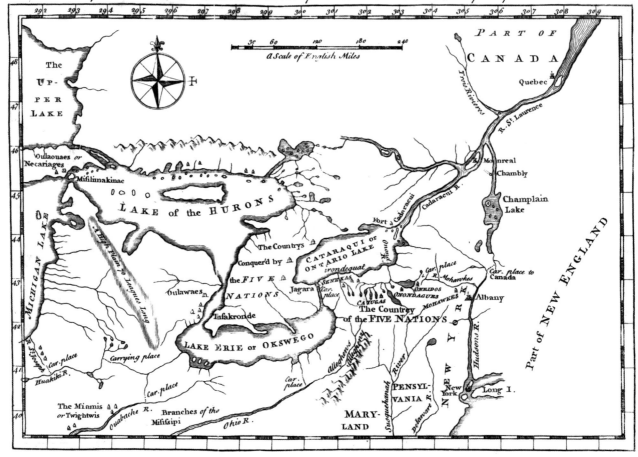

The War Club

The war club was purely a weapon, with no applications as a tool. It had ceremonial functions similar to those of a sword or rod of office, and might be used for fighting or executions. While the basic concept of a heavy weight, often of stone, on a shaft was common to many cultures, the design of war clubs varied considerably.

The tribes of the eastern coastal regions favoured a curved haft and a ball-shaped weight, sometimes with a spike, while on the Great Plains the common design was symmetrical. In the northwest, clubs might be of carved wood with no weight attached.

The war club was designed for heavy, smashing blows, possibly augmented with a puncturing action if a spike was included. This might imply a very simple style of combat, but a club could be used in a sophisticated manner by those trained in its use. In addition to big clubbing actions, the weapon could be sharply jabbed into an enemy's face. This would not be disabling, but the follow-up blow delivered as the opponent flinched might well be.

Blows with the club could be delivered to the head, shoulders and arms most easily, but a skilled warrior might feign a high blow then make a sweeping strike at the opponent's knee or the side of his leg. He might not wait to finish off an injured opponent, moving on and leaving him hobbling as an easy victim for another warrior. An injured enemy who limped away from the fight was still out of it, which might well be enough to bring victory.

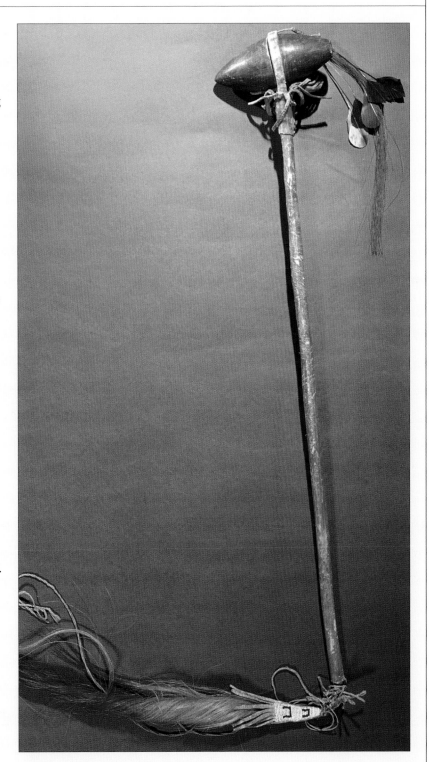

Above: The Native American war club was far more than a rock attached to a stick. Made with care and precision, it was a deadly and strangely elegant weapon.

the Huron along the St Lawrence River; this not only gave the Iroquois control of their hunting grounds but also ensured that French traders in the region had to deal with the Iroquois rather than their previous trade partners.

To the west of the Iroquois was a group of tribes known to the French as the Neutral nation for their political stance regarding other tribes. They were linguistically and culturally linked to the Iroquois and had friendlier relations with them than the nearby Algonquian-speaking tribes. Despite this, the Iroquois made war upon them from 1650 onwards, driving off or assimilating the survivors. The Erie people were similarly overrun, giving the Iroquois control of territory stretching all the way to the Great Lakes shoreline.

By 1700 the Iroquois had suffered heavily in wars against the French settlers and ceased their expansion, but their campaigns had the effect of stirring up the Ohio Valley region and driving French fur traders north to the Ottawa and other Canadian tribes.

The French and Indian War of 1756–63 involved tribes on both sides of the Appalachians and in southern Canada, and its outcome had long-term implications for the tribes of these regions. The war was, at least as far as the Europeans were concerned, between France and England, and the Treaty of Paris that ended it reflected this. Under its terms, Britain now controlled Canada and the North American continent east of the Mississippi, and Spain gained formerly French territories west of the Mississippi. French influence in the New World was reduced to some Caribbean islands.

None of this was agreed with the tribes who lived in these areas – one colonial power had defeated another and taken over its claims without regard to the people who had always lived there. The Treaty of Paris did not reflect the contribution Native American warriors had made to both sides, and, unsurprisingly perhaps, was not well received in many tribes. Nor were the colonists particularly pleased with the outcome of the war. Increased taxation to pay for it resulted in further disaffection with the Crown and ultimately a successful, if bloody, bid for independence.

Below: Brother to Tecumseh, Tenskwatawa was better known to the Europeans as simply 'The Prophet'. His teachings crossed tribal boundaries, causing great alarm among the settlers.

LEGACIES OF FRENCH SETTLEMENT

French settlers began arriving in what they called Acadia (Nova Scotia and New Brunswick) at the end of the 1500s, beginning a contested settlement in a region also partially claimed by Britain. French-speaking settlers were expelled from Acadia in 1755 after the region became a British possession. Many of them resettled in Louisiana, still owned by France at that time, and became known as Cajun.

In the intervening time, the French expanded into what is now Canada by way of the St Lawrence Valley, establishing generally good relations with the tribes there. St Lawrence offered many strategic advantages since it gave access far inland and was home to several powerful tribes. From 1600 onward, the fur trade became increasingly important, and what is now Quebec was founded as a trading post. Quebec expanded into a fortified settlement, guarding the entry point to New France, and was an obvious target for English attacks. Indeed, it was held by the British for a short time before reverting to French control, finally falling to the British in 1759.

In 1763, the French ceded their territories to the British and withdrew from the region, leaving Quebec as the main British base in the region. After withstanding attack by American revolutionary forces, Quebec became the regional capital of the new Province of Canada and later of Lower Canada when the province was divided.

When the French began settling the St Lawrence Valley, they encountered a number of

tribes who spoke languages related to Iroquoian that are collectively referred to by historians as Laurentian. These people had a semi-nomadic lifestyle similar to other tribal groups of the northeastern woodlands, building semi-permanent fortified villages and farming maize as a staple crop.

Above: The Lenape people, also known as the Delawares, were pushed out of their territory by expanding European settlement. After numerous conflicts they sided with the French against the English.

"From 1600 onward, the fur trade became increasingly important, and what is now Quebec was founded as a trading post."

The tribes of the St Lawrence Valley were typically referred to as Huron or Wyandot because of their language. They probably shared a common ancestry with the tribes of the Iroquois Confederacy,

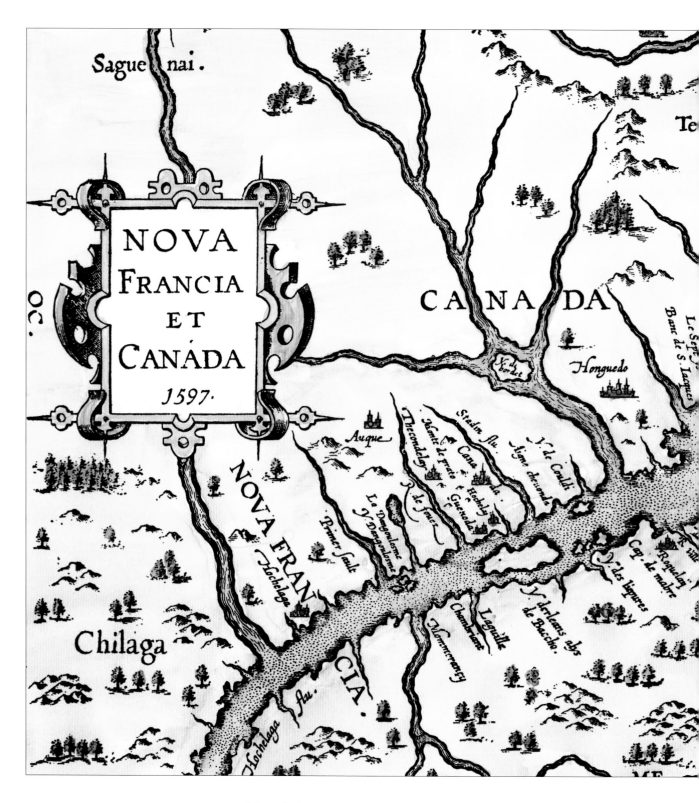

Above: New France and Canada as mapped in 1597. The St Lawrence River and its tributaries provided a conduit connecting fur trappers with the lucrative markets of Europe.

although they were a distinct culture by the time contact with Europeans occurred. Inter-tribal politics transcended such cultural commonalities and did not prevent the Iroquois from warring with their cousins. Among other causes for contention was control over the fur trade with the European settlers.

Some of the Wyandot tribes moved westward, away from the Iroquois, and settled for a time in Ontario. They were attacked again by the expanding Iroquois

PONTIAC'S WAR

For the most part, French settlers in Canada and the Ohio Valley preferred to make alliances and trade agreements with the tribes they encountered and generally considered conflict with them as bad for business. On the other hand, the English, who had newly become masters of the region (in European eyes at least) had a more imperialistic outlook. Many tribes, particularly those that had sided with the French in the recent war, were treated as subjects to be controlled rather than allies or a foreign power to be respected.

Some of the tribes of the Ohio Valley had been displaced by earlier European activity, such as the Delaware, Mingo and Shawnee. They had hoped – and been led to believe – that the British would pull back from their new homelands once they had driven out the French. When instead the newcomers began to strengthen their hold over the area with additional forts, these tribes decided to renew their hostility to Britain.

Meanwhile, an alliance was growing among the tribes of the Great Lakes region. The creation and leadership of this alliance has been credited to the Ottawa chief Pontiac, although there is some doubt about exactly how great a role he played. The plan was grand in concept but entirely workable as it devolved command to a local level and relied on a common aim rather than close cooperation. The British forts would be attacked by forces under the command of local chiefs, with additional warriors in some cases coming in from quite

from 1648. By 1650 these tribes had either been assimilated by the Iroquois or forced to move again. Some went north, some west. Many of the Huron joined the Tionontati, who were known to the French as the Tobacco Nation, but they too were attacked in turn. The remnants of the Huron Confederacy sided with the French in the French and Indian Wars and were ultimately induced to move west out of their ancestral lands into new territories in what is now Oklahoma.

distant tribes. Pontiac's own target at Detroit was to be the subject of a deception operation, with Pontiac and his followers gaining access by claiming they had come to negotiate a treaty.

"...the key to defeating the British was to cripple their logistics chain by capturing or destroying the bases that supported and protected them."

Facing page: Pontiac's forces used fire-rafts in an unsuccessful attempt to destroy two schooners based at Fort Detroit and cut off the fort's only line of communications.

Below: There was no need to maintain a constant close siege at Fort Detroit. A handful of warriors were sufficient to watch and call in others if the garrison tried to sortie or bring in supplies.

Pontiac and the other members of his alliance clearly understood the value of surprise and deception, and were well aware of the importance of seizing arsenals like that at Detroit. Although leading semi-nomadic hunters for the most part – or perhaps because of it – Pontiac realized the key to defeating the British was to cripple

their logistics chain by capturing or destroying the bases that supported and protected them.

In the event the British at Detroit were forewarned, and Pontiac was unable to launch a surprise attack. Instead he settled on a siege. Elsewhere, in May 1763 other tribes attacked British holdings and forts with mixed results. The two largest and most important forts – Pitt and Niagara – were successfully defended but several others were overrun. This placed the local settlements at the mercy of Pontiac's warriors, and they had little to offer. Similarly, garrisons were massacred after their forts fell, weakening British military strength in the region and damaging morale.

An expedition to relive Fort Pitt and drive off Pontiac's besieging force was launched in July–August 1763, advancing at a slow pace necessitated by the herds of livestock brought to feed the

garrison and the settlers who had taken shelter in the fort. Pontiac's force made a concerted attack on Fort Pitt at the end of July, trying to undermine the walls or set fire to them, but were unable to enter. They then backed off and prepared to ambush the relief column.

At the beginning of August, Pontiac's force launched an attack on the column, in what became known as the Battle of Bushy Run. Despite heavy casualties the British were able to drive off the attack and reached Fort Pitt, albeit in a depleted state. In addition to allowing the resupply of Fort Pitt, the battle improved British morale, as up to that point Pontiac's alliance had seemed invincible on their home terrain.

Attempts were similarly made to relieve Niagara in September 1763 but resulted in bloody defeat at the hands of native warriors. A relief expedition sent to assist the supply convoy was also ambushed in an area known to the British as the Devil's Hole. These actions were characterized by close-quarters combat – the fighting skills of the Native American warriors were pitted against the bayonets of the British regulars in terrain where musketry was largely ineffective.

BRITISH CAMPAIGN

The British began preparing a campaign against the alliance, but this was not launched until the spring of 1764. In the meantime Pontiac's alliance was successful against settler communities and for a time appeared to be winning the war. Although attacking a well-defended fort was a losing proposition, the Native Americans could make life very difficult for those inside with their bows and firearms. Any movement outside the fort risked attack, rendering normal activities such as hunting and farming impossible.

While those inside a large fort were reasonably safe in the short term, their position was untenable unless supplies could be brought in. In any case, the longer a siege went on the greater the chance that a successful assault would be mounted. There was also the question of prestige and influence to consider. A power whose forts were under siege yet did nothing might be perceived as weak, making uprisings or foreign attacks more likely and loosening control over the colonists in the region.

Thus, once a fort came under siege it was inevitable that sooner or later a relief expedition would be launched. There were only so many routes an organized military force with artillery and supply wagons

PONTIAC TAKING UP THE HATCHET.

could take, and naturally these were watched by Pontiac's scouts. Native American warriors could move much faster through their own lands than foreign soldiers, enabling a force to be concentrated for an ambush then moved to another promising spot.

This tactic of using a threat to a defended position to draw out a response then attack it in the open is as old as warfare itself, and was developed in the Americas independently of experience on other continents. Attempting to support the threatened forts meant playing into Pontiac's hands, enabling him to fight on his own terms as and when he chose. Instead, the British commanders chose to take the offensive. Just as the British forts were static targets, so were the villages and the crops of the tribes.

The British campaign of 1764 was hampered by disagreements between commanders and a rather liberal interpretation of orders. Nevertheless, one of the two British expeditions launched against Pontiac's alliance was successful in subduing the Delaware and Shawnee people, causing the alliance to fragment. Pontiac subsequently agreed a peace treaty with the British in 1766. This was unpopular among his former supporters, and he was murdered by a member of the Peoria tribe three years later. Pontiac's death sparked a round of conflict between local tribes, in which the Peoria people fared very badly.

It was during the siege of Fort Pitt that the idea of biological warfare against the native tribes was put forward. Up until the outbreak of Pontiac's War the British authorities had considered there was little possibility of effective resistance to their rule, and had withdrawn most of the troops sent to fight the French. Now facing a numerous and highly effective enemy, the same commanders were willing to consider any option. Orders were given to execute captive Native American warriors, but other ideas went far beyond this. Blankets from smallpox patients might be given to the tribes, it was suggested, in the hope of weakening them through disease. How effective this deliberate

> "Pontiac's death sparked a round of conflict between local tribes, in which the Peoria people fared very badly."

infection might have been is open to debate – diseases had been passed back and forth between the settlers and the native tribes for many years, and outbreaks may have had some other cause.

In the end, although Pontiac's War was a military defeat for the Native American tribes it did have important strategic outcomes. The British policy of treating the tribes as conquered people was amended, with better cooperation and more respect for native territories and values. The situation along the Ohio Valley moved a little back in the direction of what it had been while

Facing page: Symbolic actions with weapons formed an important part of Native American rhetoric, leading to expressions about 'taking up the hatchet' and burying one to symbolize the end of a conflict.

the French claimed sovereignty over the region. The war also demonstrated the capabilities of a large confederation transcending traditional boundaries and laid the groundwork for later alliances against the Europeans.

NATIVE AMERICAN vs BRITISH COLONIAL TACTICS: BUSHY RUN

On 5 August 1763, Pontiac's force attacked the head of the relief column at Bushy Run, with parties harassing the rest of the column. They faced seasoned troops, many of them Highlanders who had been serving in the Caribbean. The Royal American Regiment also supplied some of the column's defenders. Its personnel were of many nationalities and were experienced at fighting in the Americas. Notably, many of them carried tomahawks as personal weapons. The column's defenders reacted aggressively, firing volleys and charging with bayonets to disperse concentrations of attackers. These tactics had served British troops well in various colonial wars, but Pontiac's warriors simply melted away into the treeline and attacked again from another direction.

The column's commander, Colonel Henry Bouquet, changed tactics. His force formed a hollow square and made a fighting retirement to a nearby hill. There, they threw up a hasty fortification of supply sacks and whatever other cover could be found. The wounded and livestock were placed inside while Bouquet's troops defended the hilltop with accurate

musketry and the occasional aggressive counterattack.

It is obvious from the dispatches Bouquet wrote that night that he knew his force was in grave danger and probably would be overrun. His force was trapped and unable to escape, and could be gradually reduced by sharpshooters until the remainder was too weak to resist a charge. He might try to fight it out and hope Pontiac's men lost heart, but this was more than likely a losing proposition. Instead, he took advantage of Pontiac's own strategy.

Pontiac and other Native American leaders could never have heard of the great Chinese military strategist Sun Tzu, but the principles he put forward were universal. In this case, Pontiac chose to give the defenders a 'golden bridge', as Sun Tzu would have called it – an apparent way out of the death trap. He knew that men who see no escape will fight to the last but those who may be able to save themselves might attempt to retreat. If Bouquet's force could be induced to leave its defensive position it would be overrun in the forest, reducing Pontiac's losses enormously. Even if only part of the British force fled, the rest would be weakened and easily overrun.

However, Bouquet correctly deduced this strategy and played to Pontiac's expectations. He sent some of his troops out of the defensive position as if they were taking advantage of the perceived weakness of Pontiac's men on the side nearest Fort Pitt. This force hooked around Pontiac's flank ready to attack once he committed his men to the final assault. As they did so, they ran into determined

Facing page: In response to a 1500-strong expedition beginning in October 1764, Pontiac agreed a peace parlay and returned large numbers of captives taken in the war.

Below: Colonel Henry Bouquet correctly predicted Pontiac's expectations and exploited them. A lesser commander would have been disastrously out-generalled at Bushy Run.

B. West inv.ᵗ   Canot sculp.

The Indians delivering up the English Captives to Colonel Bouquet
near his Camp at the Forks of Muskingum in North America in Nov.ᵇᵉʳ 176

Native American Strategy: Fear, Deception and Stealth

Above: The Anishinabeg people were known to the French as Ojibwa and the English as Chippewa.

The effective use of deception is an integral part of modern warfare, and history abounds with tales of clever ruses and surprise attacks. The simplest example is the stealthy ambush of a convoy or patrol, or a force sneaking into position near a target under cover of darkness to strike as soon as there is sufficient light. Stealthy tactics such as these were used whenever possible. At Point Pelee, a force of Ottawas caught a small British force by surprise and captured them along with their boats. However, deception could be used in far more sophisticated ways.

The stratagem used by Pontiac at Detroit was straightforward, but Native American tribes could be highly inventive. At Fort Michilimackinac, a party of Ojibwa warriors played a game of lacrosse close to the fort, chasing a 'stray' ball inside the defences before launching their attack. This might not have worked if the tribe had not played many similar games before in view of the fort, creating a sense of normalcy that made a reaction unlikely. In the event, the warriors who got inside armed themselves with weapons that had been smuggled in by female members of their tribe and were able to overwhelm the garrison before effective resistance could be mounted.

Massacres were commonplace when a fort was overrun, even when a garrison had surrendered on terms. Those who were captured might be burned or tortured to death. Fear was an effective weapon, weakening the resolve of any British soldiers who might venture into the tribal lands to retake their lost forts.

resistance rather than the wavering defence they expected, facing a volley of double-shotted muskets at close range. Fired on then charged from the rear, Pontiac's men were caught between the flanking force and a counter-charge from the fort, and they scattered after a hard fight.

The meeting between Pontiac and Bouquet was no mere skirmish in the forest, even though the numbers involved were not great by European standards. It was a clash between expert warriors of both cultures commanded by leaders who understood one another's tactics. The immediate outcome was the relief of Fort Pitt, which would otherwise have fallen, with catastrophic consequences for the British occupation of the Ohio Valley.

In the longer term, the losses incurred at Bushy Run were unacceptable. If every fight with the British – win or lose – was as costly then the Native American nations would cease to exist. Pontiac thus began exploring the possibility of a negotiated peace rather than seeking outright victory.

THE WESTERN CONFEDERACY AND THE NORTHWEST INDIAN WAR

One outcome of the American Revolution for the tribes of North America was that they would now contend with the agenda of the colonists – now the fledgling United States of America – rather than their colonial backers. The USA had far fewer resources to bring to bear on an issue, but it was focussed on expansion rather than making money from trade or other economic activity in the Americas.

Where previously the colonial outposts of a distant power might find trade more lucrative than territorial conquest, conflict over land was now inevitable.

Movement towards unified opposition to European incursions began before Pontiac's War, but cooperation began in earnest after the American Revolution. The alliance often known as the Western Confederacy (as well

"If every fight with the British – win or lose – was as costly then the Native American nations would cease to exist."

as by various other names) was first formed in 1786 and came to incorporate a large number of tribes, many of whom had no history of cooperation. Some had been enemies in the past, but differences meant little in the face of the new threat.

The Western Confederacy drew in confederations of tribes including the Seven Nations of Canada and the Iroquois, the Illinois Confederacy of the Mississippi Valley and the Wabash Confederacy of tribes living on the Wabash River. However, in many cases villages and groups joined the confederacy rather than a tribe as a whole. Many tribes were insufficiently unified to make such a commitment, and decisions to join or not were made at the local level.

The war opened with an escalation of the raids that

Above: After Harmar's defeat, steam rising from the heads of dead US soldiers was said to be reminiscent of a pumpkin field, giving rise to the battle's name among the tribes.

Facing page: Arthur St Clair began his military career in the British army and later fought against it in the War of Independence. He was forced to resign his commission after his disastrous defeat.

had already been occurring sporadically, possibly with the approval and support of agents appointed by the British crown. The newly independent United States retaliated with assaults on Native American settlements, notably those of the Shawnee people. Some villages were attacked while their warriors were away raiding and were easily overrun. Settlements and crops were burned in the now familiar pattern of retaliation, but this only had the effect of escalating hostilities.

In late 1790 the first large-scale response was made by the USA. Commanded by General Josiah Harmar, a force of poorly trained regular soldiers and militia, accompanied by some light artillery, advanced along the Great Miami River. Informed by their scouts of exactly where the column was headed, the local tribes, led by Chief Little Turtle of the Miami people, adopted an 'elastic defence' as it might be called in modern

military doctrine, and pulled back from their villages.

As the expedition advanced further into Native American territory, elements of it were drawn into ambushes while the main force was over-cautious and failed to support its detachments. Both cavalry and infantry were at times induced to chase handfuls of Native American sharpshooters into terrain where they could be isolated and overwhelmed, with the superior mobility of the tribal warriors enabling them to concentrate at the critical point. The firepower and artillery of the US regulars was offset by the clumsiness of their force and the crafty tactics of the Native American leaders, who refused to commit their warriors where the regulars could concentrate fire on them.

The expedition was defeated at what became known as the Battle of the Pumpkin Fields, when a large detachment was picked to pieces while the main US force remained in defensive array and failed to support it. The survivors rejoined the expedition and the force as a whole retreated. The defeat of General Harmar's expedition had important strategic consequences. Heartened by their victory, the tribes of the confederation increased the scope and intensity of their attacks, hitting settlements across the whole region. More warriors came to join the war, and Chief Little Turtle became a renowned leader.

In 1791, General Arthur St Clair was placed in command of a renewed campaign, although the resources at his disposal were limited. Despite the folly of

sending raw troops and untrained militia into the wilderness to fight the tribes that lived there – as demonstrated the previous year – St Clair set out into the Wabash Valley. His force was attacked in its poorly fortified camp by a force of about 1000 Native American warriors. Despite parity of numbers and a defensive position, the US force collapsed and was quickly overrun with very heavy casualties. The battle, known as St Clair's Defeat, was notable for the use of sharpshooters to nullify US artillery by picking off their crews. Highly mobile tactics were used to flank enemy volley lines and to evade bayonet charges by falling back into the nearby woods before attacking again.

In the wake of this victory, which would be the largest they ever achieved against the US, the Native American leaders began to consider negotiating a peace settlement. While the possibilities were being discussed, raids continued and the US constructed additional forts in an attempt to methodically gain control of the region. This was countered by a raid to destroy a concentration of packhorses that could be used to maintain the supply route between the forts.

The tribes of the Western Confederacy were unable to agree

Below: The later stages of St Clair's Defeat took the form of a mopping-up operation as scattered US troops were run down and killed.

Close-quarters Combat

Above: The Europeans' weaponry advantage could be offset by dashing in close. An opponent could be thrown to the ground, stabbed with a knife or simply held for an ally to strike.

Once close combat began there was no time to go through the complex process of reloading a flintlock firearm. A combatant who still had a loaded musket or perhaps a pistol might get a shot off, but for the most part firearms were useless at short ranges.

The Native American warrior was lightly equipped and much more capable offensively than defensively. Some tribes used shields to protect against arrows, and various forms of light armour were in use in some regions, but for the most part the warrior relied on speed and aggression to eliminate his enemy before he suffered much harm. He might block a blow with his weapon or slap aside the thrust of a bayonet or spear with an empty hand, but for the most part his aim was to move quickly among his enemies, striking at whatever targets presented themselves, rather than becoming locked into a formal exchange of attack and defence.

The Native American warrior was a hunter and a fighter rather than a soldier, and his tactics resembled those of his mammoth-hunting ancestors. He was vulnerable to any blow, and he knew it. He might work with friends to distract an enemy so that another warrior could strike him down from the side or rear. However, he would take risks if necessary and would be concerned about the opinion of his peers if he was seen to be hanging back.

A close-quarters fight was a frantic scramble. A European soldier armed with musket and bayonet might be dealt with by grabbing the barrel of his weapon and stabbing him with a knife, or by a well-timed rush with a war club or tomahawk. Weapons or even rocks might be thrown, and any enemy could be wrestled to the ground and finished with knives.

Above: Defeat at the Battle of Fallen Timbers forced the Northwestern Confederacy to accept a peace treaty ceding vast tracts of land to the fledgling United States.

on the terms they would demand from the US, so the conflict continued into 1793. During this time the US – which had lost about a quarter of its available troops under St Clair – trained a new

> *"At the end of 1793, the Legion of the United States advanced and began building fortified positions."*

force that might stand a chance against the native tribes. This was named the Legion of the United States, and was formed on the basis of combined arms tactics, with

sub-units all containing a mix of infantry, artillery and cavalry.

At the end of 1793, the Legion of the United States advanced and began building fortified positions. These were duly attacked, but although the logistics support network was damaged by the loss of many pack animals the forts held out. The following year, Little Turtle and Blue Jacket confronted around 2000 US troops at the Battle of Fallen Timbers on the Maumee River. Numbers were about equal at 1500–2000 on each side, but the US Legion was a far better fighting force than the ill-trained and nervous troops of St Clair's expedition. Bayonet charges by infantry and flanking attacks by cavalry were successful on this occasion, driving the Native American force from the field.

Forced to sue for peace, the confederacy gave up much of what is now Ohio and the surrounding states at the 1795 Treaty of Greenville. US settlers began moving into the region in greater numbers, and although resistance continued, many chiefs – including Little Turtle – discouraged further conflict. The British had managed to retain Fort Detroit despite their defeat in the American Revolution, and up until 1796 British agents at the fort continued to incite Native American warriors to harass the new United States. The year after the Northwest Indian War ended, Fort Detroit was handed over to the US.

Below: The Treaty of Greenville was controversial among the Native American tribes. Opponents said that it ceded lands the signatories were not empowered to give away.

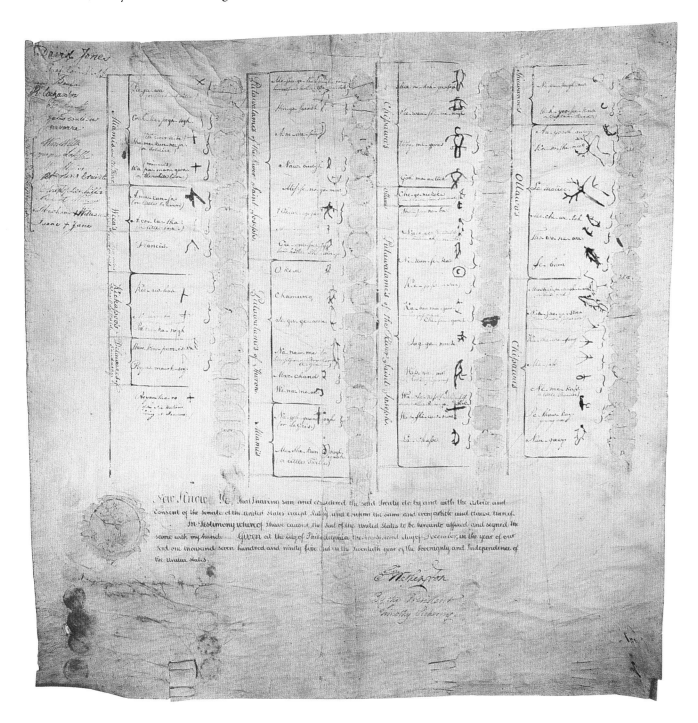

Fortification in the Americas

By the 1600s, Europeans were building sophisticated artillery forts to defend against one another. Gone were the high castle walls; instead a complex system of ramparts, ditches and outworks protected artillery emplacements and infantry positions. Defence was less about keeping enemies out than making it prohibitively expensive in terms of casualties to get into a defended place, using interlocking fields of fire to slaughter enemy troops struggling through the defences.

Such fortifications were rare in the Americas before the Civil War, since most enemies would not have artillery. Defences tended to be simpler, consisting of a wall or palisade of logs possibly augmented by a ditch or earth rampart. Artillery might well be incorporated into these defences, but it would normally face attack by infantry rather than bombardment by cannon and did not require heavy protection. Similarly, Native American villages were typically defended by a wooden palisade if they had any fortification at all.

In this environment, a wall or palisade was an effective defence. It would stop bullets and arrows and prevented enemies from coming to close quarters. More importantly, it restricted access to critical supplies such as gunpowder, food and ammunition, and gave the garrison a safe place to rest and recover. While very basic by the standards of European warfare, the log forts of the Americas were invaluable to their owners, but they were also at times a liability.

A fort was static, and could be cut off by interdicting its supply route. If messengers were intercepted, relief would not materialize and the garrison were on their own. A large fort or a fortified settlement might survive a siege of this sort, but the small outposts scattered throughout the Ohio Valley and elsewhere were often held only by a handful of men with very limited resources. Without assistance their outlook was bleak.

Below: Tecumseh is often depicted in the uniform of a British officer, but this may have been an affectation of the artist.

TECUMSEH'S WAR

The conflict that became known as Tecumseh's War took place against the backdrop of the War of 1812. This was another 'white man's war' that involved the Native American nations. Britain and the United States came into conflict as a result of international politics, but were quite willing to make common cause with Native Americans if this furthered their objectives. For their part, the Native American nations of the Ohio Valley region hoped that British support would enable them to drive out the settlers moving into the region and reclaim it for their own.

Among the Native American leaders of the time was Tecumseh, a chief of the Shawnee people. He lost his father in battle against colonial militia from Virginia and had taken

part in raids against the settlers. Tecumseh fought in the Northwest Indian War and wanted no part in the Treaty of Greenville that ended it.

From 1805, Tecumseh's brother Lalawethika emerged as a religious leader preaching a return to the traditional way of life and the rejection of European influences. Tecumseh became involved in expanding their following but was more interested in the political possibilities than the spiritual aspects. He saw the religious teachings of his brother as a way to create a new tribal confederation that might be able to oppose the United States. The religious movement was centred on a new village on the banks of the River Tippecanoe, which became known

as Prophetstown. Lalawethika had taken the name Tenskwatawa, but the 'white man' knew him as The Prophet and naturally referred to his base in similar manner. The population came from various tribes, drawn by the teachings of Lalawethika and the diplomatic overtures of Tecumseh.

As the US tried to induce tribes in the region to sell more land, Tecumseh countered with arguments that land was not owned by any one tribe and could therefore not be sold by it; all tribes had to agree to give up the territory of any. When this failed, he tried openly threatening tribal leaders who agreed to the sale. Questionable treaties such as that signed at Fort Wayne in 1809 were rejected by

Above: Tecumseh warned his brother not to fight while he was away, but was ignored. The resulting Battle of Tippecanoe was a mortal blow to Tecumseh's confederacy.

Tecumseh's followers, leading to a rapid increase in tensions.

The confederation, and Tecumseh in particular, was seen as a real threat to US ambitions in the region, and in November 1811 US troops marched on Prophetstown while Tecumseh was away on a diplomatic mission to the Creek nation. They were met by Lalawethika and his followers, who had recently reversed their position on eschewing European technology such as firearms and obtained weaponry from British traders. Lalawethika's followers attacked the US camp in what became known as the Battle of Tippecanoe, but were defeated. Prophetstown was burned down and food supplies destroyed.

This was a heavy blow to Tecumseh's confederation, but the outbreak of the War of 1812 offered new possibilities. He led his followers to join other Native Americans fighting alongside the British and assisted in the capture of Detroit. Tecumseh had agreed to assist the British in return for their support in reclaiming his home region for the native tribes, but this never came to pass. His force retreated into Canada alongside its British allies and was brought to action at the Battle of the Thames in October 1813.

Tecumseh was killed during the battle, and as might be expected in the case of such a

THE BLACKFOOT CONFEDERACY

The Blackfoot were a nomadic people, living in tipis constructed from hides stretched over a frame of poles. Tipis were used by the Great Plains tribes instead of the wigwams popular elsewhere, largely as a result of the available materials. A tipi was also relatively easy to dismantle and move.

It is thought that the Blackfoot migrated westward into the northern Great Plains from the northeastern woodlands, by way of the region north of the Great Lakes. Conflict with tribes already settled in the region kept them moving until they established their own territory in what is now North and South Dakota.

The name Siksika, loosely translated to English as 'Blackfoot', actually meant 'those with black moccasins'. Whereas most tribes famous warrior there were many claims to have been the person that killed him. Political careers were enhanced by such boasts, but there is no clear indication of who actually killed Tecumseh and who was merely trying to take the credit.

His confederation collapsed and with the end of the War of 1812 there was no strong ally for the Native American nations of the Ohio basin.

Left: Tecumseh's warriors guarded the British flank on the Thames, and fought on despite overwhelming odds when the British force collapsed.

Below: The Blackfoot originally used sleds called *travois* pulled by dogs to carry their possessions. The horse greatly increased their mobility and military power.

"After 1730, the Blackfoot began to make use of horses and the animal became very important in their culture."

made their moccasins from new hides that gave them a beige colour, the Siksika people used old hides that had previously been part of a tipi. Smoke exiting the tipi via a hole at the top blackened the hides, giving the Siksika people's footwear its distinctive feature.

The Siksika were nomadic, hunting buffalo and deer for food and clothing. Hides were sewn with buffalo sinew to make highly decorated tunics, leggings and robes that were worn in colder weather.

Although the buffalo was their primary food source, they were adept at taking other game and would also forage for wild plants. They did not practise agriculture, although they grew tobacco.

As plains hunters, the Siksika favoured the bow and also used it in war. For personal combat, spears and war clubs were the weapons of choice, with knives as a back-up in an emergency. Most warriors would have seen their knife as a tool rather than a weapon, but some were skilled at fighting with it. Hide-covered shields were also used by some warriors.

After 1730, the Blackfoot began to make use of horses, and the animal became very important in their culture. Stealing one in a raid was a worthy accomplishment, and owning several was a sign of prestige and source of power.

Below: Raiding other tribes for horses demonstrated the prowess of a warrior in a manner that strengthened his own people while depriving an enemy of a critical resource.

The Tomahawk

Perhaps the most iconic weapon of the Native American warrior was the tomahawk. Relatively simple to make, with a blade that could be of metal or stone, it was used as a tool far more often than a weapon. Tomahawks were often decorated with feathers, medicine bundles or carvings, especially those intended for ceremonial functions. The tomahawk was extremely versatile, combining the capabilities of a hammer, axe and blade. It could be used for relatively fine work or delivering powerful blows either to an enemy or in more mundane applications such as cutting wood.

In combat, the tomahawk could be thrown but was normally used in the hand, with part of the haft protruding below the warrior's fist. This section could be used to hook an enemy or his weapon and drag

him forward, setting up for a jabbing action with the other end of the haft. The cutting blade, even if made of stone, was sharp enough to wound if simply brought into contact with an enemy's flesh and dragged across it. A blow with body weight behind it would punch deep into the opponent or could smash bones by sheer force of impact.

The tomahawk was sufficiently useful and versatile that it was adopted as a tool and a weapon by many colonists, and remains in service today as a military tool that can serve as a weapon if needed.

Below: Throwing a tomahawk effectively meant imparting enough rotation that the weapon struck blade first.

Left: Early tomahawks were simply small axes and could just as accurately be referred to as hatchets. Later designs evolved features designed primarily for combat.

Right: The Cree were well aware of the value of trade with the newly arrived Europeans, and formed the Iron Confederacy to take control of it.

"Contact with Europeans resulted in disease outbreaks, notably smallpox, which weakened the Blackfoot and gave their enemies an advantage over them."

Horses rapidly became vital to success in hunting and warfare, as the tribes that adopted their use could range more widely and strike more swiftly than those that did not.

Contact with Europeans came around 1750, when traders from the Hudson's Bay Company established posts along the Saskatchewan River. Blackfoot parties visited the posts to trade buffalo hides and beaver pelts. Contact with Europeans resulted in disease outbreaks, notably smallpox, which weakened the Blackfoot and gave their enemies an advantage over them.

The Blackfoot Confederacy did not become involved in the

wars between the tribes of the
Great Plains and the United States
of America, although there were
incidents of violence. Despite this,
the Blackfoot were victims of the
deliberate extermination of the
bison herds they depended on. The
loss of their traditional food source
forced the Blackfoot to adopt a
settled agricultural lifestyle, for

which they had little aptitude.
Those that did not migrate
northwards into Canada became
dependent on US government
assistance as they made the
transition to a new way of life.

THE CREE CONFEDERACY

The 'Cree' called themselves
Kenistenoag, but this was

corrupted and shortened to Cree
by French traders. They migrated
southwards from sub-Arctic
Canada to the Great Plains and the
northeast woodlands. Those that
moved to a new woodland home
retained much of their original
lifestyle, living in birch-bark
wigwams and fishing from canoes
made of the same material.

Above: The Plains Cree became dependent upon the bison for food and raw materials, which forced them into conflict with other tribes when the bison herds became depleted.

The Plains Cree had to adapt to their new environment, becoming nomadic hunters living in tipis. Like the Blackfoot, they spoke Algonquian, but this common heritage did not prevent the two from being enemies at times. The Cree used similar weapons and wore similar clothing to the Blackfoot, and also adopted the horse and the gun when they became available.

The Cree appointed different chiefs for war and for peace, playing to the strengths of individuals. The office of war chief was a temporary one, possibly for a single expedition or throughout a longer conflict, after which control reverted to the peace chiefs. Together with their allies, notably the Assiniboine, the Cree formed the 'Iron Confederacy' as a political and military alliance. In addition to warfare, the confederacy was a powerful factor in the fur trade, forcing others to go through the confederacy's traders when dealing with the Hudson's Bay Company and Northwest Company.

It was long believed that the Cree migration from sub-Arctic Canada was made in order to take advantage of the fur trade to Europe, but it is likely that the movement had already begun when Europeans first arrived. Be that as it may, the Cree understood the value of controlling the fur trade and were prepared to fight for it.

The power of the Iron Confederacy came mainly from control of the fur trade, and the fortunes of the confederacy declined with it. As the numbers of bison were reduced by over-hunting, conflicts broke out over the bison themselves and violations of tribal territory by hunting parties who had no alternative if they were not to go hungry. The need to follow the bison herds resulted in conflict with the Blackfoot, culminating in the Battle of Belly River in 1870. The fighting took the form of a protracted exchange of gunfire, escalating as more warriors from both sides joined in. Ultimately the Blackfoot outmanoeuvred their opponents and were able to fire into the Cree positions from high ground. The Cree suffered heavy casualties as they attempted to retreat, and sued for peace soon afterward. This was cemented by the adoption of Poundmaker, a promising young Cree, as the son of the Blackfoot chief Crowfoot.

THE NORTHWEST REBELLION

As soon as Europeans landed in the Americas it became inevitable that interbreeding would occur. The offspring of these unions usually remained with their mother and joined her culture. Known as Métis, among other names, these mixed-race children

Below: The Métis developed a unique culture that intermingled influences from the local tribes with the resourcefulness and self-reliance of backwoods trappers and hunters.

Facing page: Poundmaker not only had a unique talent for herding bison but also symbolized the end to conflict between the Cree and the Blackfoot.

Below: Louis Riel led an uprising of the Métis against the Canadian government that coincided with the plans of the Cree nation.

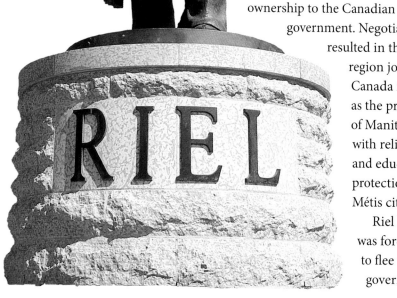

formed a cultural bridge between the Native American people and the newcomers. They were not always accepted, but over time the fur trapping settlements came to include an increasing number of Métis, and it developed a culture that was neither settler nor native but a melding of the two.

The Métis became a distinct cultural group with their own interests that in some cases diverged from those of the settlers or the native tribes. They experienced what was in many ways a repeat of what had happened to the Native American tribes – the new government of Canada began buying land from the Métis and settlers encroached upon their home territories with or without official approval.

The Métis resisted as best they could, but a confrontation became inevitable. Under the leadership of Louis Riel, the Métis formed a provisional government and declared that since the Hudson's Bay Company no longer controlled the region it could not transfer ownership to the Canadian government. Negotiations resulted in the region joining Canada in 1870 as the province of Manitoba, with religious and educational protections for Métis citizens.

Riel himself was forced to flee when government

troops arrived, and over time the Métis became concerned that the Canadian government was not inclined to respect the terms of the Manitoba Act that guaranteed their way of life would be preserved. In 1885 an armed uprising took place, again led by Riel, and at the same time the Cree took up arms against the Canadian government under the leadership of Poundmaker.

Poundmaker gained his name from a special talent he possessed. Perhaps as a result of his parentage – his father was a medicine man – he could attract buffalo into a pound with the assistance of spirits. Poundmaker was adopted in 1873 by Chief Crowfoot of the Blackfoot, ending a period of conflict between the two confederations. He favoured peaceful relations with the Canadian government and was receptive to a treaty ceding land, but over time he became disaffected when the government did not seem to respect the treaty.

Suffering from hunger as the bison became increasingly scarce, the Cree left their reservations and headed for Battleford to seek help. The townsfolk feared an attack was imminent and fled to a nearby fort. Troops were despatched in response to telegrams requesting assistance, although the peaceful intentions of Poundmaker and his followers were established before that force arrived. The Cree were blamed for looting that had occurred in Battleford after the population fled, although in truth they were probably not responsible.

A series of incidents followed, largely resulting from the

desperation of the starving Cree, and in May 1885 government troops attacked Poundmaker's camp at Cut Knife Creek. Some 392 men, supported by two artillery pieces and a Gatling gun, were deployed against a total population of about 1500 Cree and friendly tribes. Poundmaker anticipated the attack and handed over leadership to Fine Day, who was to serve as war chief. Fine Day's tactics were to hit and run in small groups, spreading confusion among the Canadian troops. Many were inexperienced and over-estimated the force they faced, and could not find targets to shoot at. The Cree made expert use of concealment, sneaking close to make their attacks and then disappearing. Despite a lack of ammunition and being outnumbered – and facing artillery fire – the Cree forced the Canadian troops to withdraw,

and it was only the intervention of Poundmaker that prevented them from being massacred as they struggled through difficult terrain. Poundmaker asked the Cree warriors not to pursue, and although Fine Day was the war chief and had command, his request was heeded.

The Cree were not looking for a fight – they just wanted the government to give them more food. The government also did not want conflict. Against the backdrop of the NorthWest Rebellion, tensions were running high and the commander of the relief force, Colonel Otter, launched the attack in disobedience of his orders. However, once begun the fighting continued unabated.

After the defeat of the Métis at Batoche in May, the Cree fought on for a time against the Canadian government. Canadian troops had

Below: Despite a gallant fight and a firm grasp of modern infantry tactics, the Cree simply could not sustain their war and Poundmaker was forced to surrender.

Scalping

The practice of scalping enemies, usually for trophies, was known in Europe and Asia long before contact with the Americas. Opinions are divided as to whether scalping was practised in the Americas before the arrival of Europeans. If it was, then this was on a small scale and probably for ritual purposes.

The taking of scalps was a convenient way to prove that enemies had been killed, as scalps were much easier to carry than severed heads. It was possible to tell from the hair whether the victim was European or Native American, which was useful to settler groups using local warriors to fight proxy wars for them.

Bounties were paid for scalps of the target group, which might be another European faction one year and a native tribe the next, depending on local politics. The increased use of metal knives made scalping easy, and a successful warband could make a great deal of money in a short time this way.

Over time, the practice spread and became part of Native American culture. Scalps were taken as trophies even when no bounties were on offer, and came to be part of rituals of vengeance. A family that had lost a member to another tribe would be presented with the scalp of one of the enemy to show that retribution had been carried out.

It is not possible to say for certain whether scalping was practised in North America before the coming of the European settlers, but it is clear that it became established as a widespread practice – so widespread that some Europeans scalped particularly hated enemies among themselves – as a result of scalp bounties. Europeans may or may not have brought the practice of scalping to the New World, but they definitely encouraged it.

Left: The taking of scalps served many purposes, some of them religious. Scalping for bounties was introduced by the Europeans but came to be thought of as a Native American custom.

learned to respect their opponents after the disaster at Cut Knife Creek and were keen to avoid what Major-General Strange, leading a force against Cree under Big Bear, described as 'committing Custer'.

Big Bear made a stand at Frenchman's Butte, creating a fortified position using rifle pits dug into the hillside. These were attacked with artillery fire, but the Canadians were unable to make a successful advance. Attempts at outflanking Big Bear's position were defeated by mobile detachments, and an infiltration into the Canadians' rear eventually caused Major-General Strange to order a withdrawal.

members on both sides of the US–Canadian border. The Métis are recognized as a people separate from the First Nations and the descendants of Europeans. The Inuit are Arctic-dwelling people found in Alaska and Greenland as well as Canada. Their harsh environment resulted in the development of a different culture to their southern neighbours.

The Inuit were late arrivals on the North American continent, and with the more temperate lands filling up with potentially hostile tribes they remained in the far north. Their languages diverged over time but were all part of the same Inuit–Aleut family that is

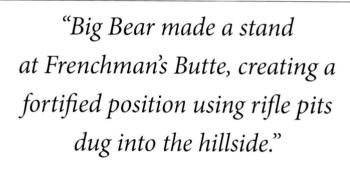

> *"Big Bear made a stand at Frenchman's Butte, creating a fortified position using rifle pits dug into the hillside."*

After a defeat at Loon Lake in June, the Cree could no longer fight on. Poundmaker tried to make peace but was arrested and imprisoned. His adoptive father Crowfoot was able to obtain a release, but Poundmaker died soon afterward as a result of unhealthy conditions during his prison term.

THE INUIT
Today, there are three broad groups of aboriginal peoples in Canada. Most Native American groups have come to refer to themselves as First Nations, and many of these groups have

quite distinct from other North American language families such as proto-Iroquoian or proto-Algonquian.

Inuit were nomadic, moving to follow the available game. In summer they lived in tents made from hides stretched over a wooden frame. Wood was hard to come by and was often driftwood salvaged wherever it could be found. In winter, igloos built out of snow blocks provided shelter. Using the only readily available building material, a skilled builder could put an igloo together in as little as half an hour.

There were exceptions to this general rule. Those Inuit living in regions with more vegetation, notably in the west of the continent, built semi-subterranean huts by digging a hole and constructing a wooden roof covered with turf. These semi-permanent dwellings provided good shelter in the winter when the tribe was not on the move.

The Inuit could not practise agriculture, and in some regions they could only gather edible plants for a short time in summer. Therefore the hunt had to provide all of their needs. Inuit hunted on

the ice for seal, walrus and even whale, and on land for birds and animals. Some tribes were almost totally dependent on the caribou while others hunted a greater variety of animals. Fishing was also important; it could be done from a canoe in summer or through an ice hole in winter.

The harpoon was one of the Inuit's most important weapons. A wounded seal might escape under ice or swim away before dying, but by using a harpoon with a line attached it could be brought back and a sealskin float ensured the prey did not sink. Inuit harpoons

were sophisticated items, with different heads used for each type of prey. They could also be used for fishing.

Most Inuit tools and weapons used bone or stone tips. The ulu was a knife typically made with a stone blade attached to a handle of antler or walrus ivory. It could serve as a weapon at need but was also a tool for skinning animals and carrying out a variety of other tasks.

The Inuit were, on the whole, a peaceable people. By choosing to live in such a harsh environment they reduced the amount of competition they faced and thus

Above: The skills of fishing and hunting sea mammals along the shore lent themselves less readily to warfare than hunting on the plains or in the forests, but the Inuit had few enemies and rarely needed to fight.

did not need a warrior culture like some of the more southerly tribes. The most common threat faced by Inuit was dangerous animals such as a wounded caribou or a polar bear, and these were dealt with using the skills of the hunt.

However, the Inuit could and did fight. When the Norsemen landed in Newfoundland they quickly came to despise the 'Skraelings' (wretches), as they called the locals, and dismissed them as Stone Age primitives. Their weapons and tools were indeed made from stone, but they were anything but primitive. After a period of mistreatment by the Europeans, the Inuit waged war on the Norsemen, besieging them in their camp in much the same way that more southerly tribes made the area around European forts untenable.

Ultimately, the warriors of the Inuit drove the Europeans from their land and went back to their peaceful existence. The tribes to their south were probably unaware of the incident at the time. Europeans eventually came to the Arctic but again the harsh conditions protected the Inuit better than any warriors could. Europeans did not want to settle where the Inuit lived, so there was little or no conflict. As a result, their way of life survived when other indigenous cultures were destroyed or altered beyond recognition.

Tribes of the Great Plains

To the west of the Appalachian Mountains lies the Interior Lowland, through which the Missouri and Ohio rivers flow to join the Mississippi. To the west of the lowlands lie the Great Plains, stretching north to south from the Mackenzie River to the Rio Grande.

Much of the Great Plains lie at quite high altitudes. The Rocky Mountains to the west create a rain shadow effect, causing moist air from the Pacific Ocean to deposit rain on the westward side of the mountains and resulting in a semi-arid climate for the Great Plains.

There are areas of high land, many with extensive forestation, but the Great Plains are for the most part characterized by dry prairie and grassland.

The climate of the Great Plains can be highly changeable. Winters tend to be cold and summers warm, but local variations are considerable. When the Chinook, a warm wind from the Rocky Mountains, blows, the temperature can rise rapidly in a very short period of time.

Life here was very different to the northeastern woodlands or the Ohio Valley. Timber was available for construction, but for most Native Americans permanent structures were not an option. Tribes needed to be constantly on the move to follow the hunt. This was difficult before the horse was introduced to the Americas, and as a result the Great Plains were sparsely populated until the 1600s. After this, tribes began to move westwards – or were forced to do so – and the Great Plains were settled.

Left: Combat between warriors of the Sioux and Blackfoot, showing the traditional weapons of lance and tomahawk in use alongside firearms.

Above: In September 1887, the Indian Agent at the Montana Crow reservation mistook gunfire in celebration of a victory over the Blackfoot for an attack, triggering a war between the Crow and the US government.

RESERVATIONS AND INDIAN AGENTS

The idea of creating reserved areas for Native American tribes originated well before the independence of the United States, and by the mid-1760s a framework was in place for land purchases and the rules governing them. These were not always followed, and in 1824 the Office of Indian Affairs was set up to rationalize the complex situation that had arisen. The Office of Indian Affairs was preceded by the Office of Indian Trade, set up in 1806, which was narrower in its remit and primarily concerned with the fur trade. The underlying concept was that the patchwork of local agreements and informal situations that had – or had not – come to be locally accepted would be replaced by treaties between the US government and the tribes, treating each tribe as a sovereign state.

Whether or not the treaties were negotiated in good faith, in many cases they were quickly abrogated or replaced by new deals under which the tribes received much smaller reservations. Similarly, the assistance that should have been granted in moving the tribes to their new homes was patchy and often totally inadequate, resulting in great hardships.

Life was often difficult on the reservations, since the best land was often given to – or taken by – white settlers. Several conflicts arose because a tribe could not support itself on the land that had been granted to it, forcing tribe members to leave the reservation that in turn triggered military intervention.

'Indian Agents' were appointed as liaison between the tribes and the US government. Theirs was a thankless task if performed honourably, and an opportunity for embezzlement for those who were so inclined. The support granted to tribes was thin enough without agents skimming for their own profit, and turnover in agents was high. They were expected to keep the tribes from causing trouble and to implement Federal policy within their jurisdiction, which was a task as difficult as it was unpopular.

> *"...the assistance that should have been granted in moving the tribes to their new homes was patchy and often totally inadequate..."*

In Canada, a similar system of agents was implemented, although the Department of Indian Affairs was not formed until 1880. In both Canada and the USA these agents wielded sufficient power that they were often able to usurp decision-making processes that were supposed to be handled by tribal leaders.

THE PAWNEE

The Pawnee were resident on the Great Plains in the 1500s, and probably before. Unlike later arrivals they were sedentary, living for most of the year in earth lodges and growing crops. The Pawnee did hunt buffalo, sending out parties who lived in temporary camps using tipis, but these hunts

Below: Carbines were favoured by many warriors over rifles, as they were much handier on horseback and not significantly less accurate on foot.

"...rituals included human sacrifice, which was practised by some but by no means all tribes."

were short in duration and did not involve moving the whole tribe.

The Pawnee were not a particularly warlike people, and suffered from encroachment by those that moved onto the plains. Indeed, so many Pawnee were taken as captives and sold as slaves that the term for a native American slave in Canada was 'panis', a corruption of the tribe's name. Slavery was common among the indigenous people of North America long before Europeans arrived. Captives taken in war

might consider themselves lucky to be enslaved; the alternative was usually ritual torture or at best a quick execution. Some were adopted into the tribe however, either to replace losses or because they had impressed their captors.

The Pawnee did have a warrior class within their society, along with hunters and medicine men. The latter were of two types: shamans who dealt with the spirit world and priests who led the many ceremonies carried out by the tribe. These rituals included human sacrifice, which was practised by some but by no means all tribes. Typically the subject was a slave or captive of a type suited to the ritual.

War captives were favoured by some tribes, but for the Pawnee Morning Star ritual performed in

Below: A Pawnee camp in the Platte Valley in Nebraska. The Pawnee generally allied themselves with the US government against their traditional Native American enemies.

The Lance

The spear is one of the most basic yet effective weapons for hunting and war, and was one of the earliest to be developed by the Native American tribes. Once the horse became widely available, longer spears were introduced. It is customary to refer to a spear-like weapon used from horseback as a lance, although the distinction is blurry.

The lance initially had a stone tip, and although metal spearheads were later introduced a workable lance could still be furnished by anyone with access to a suitable material such as flint. The lance gave a rider increased reach and was capable of thrusting in any direction. Native Americans used their spears from horseback much as they would on foot, stabbing the target as they rode by, but out of reach.

In the buffalo hunt, the lance was used to wound an animal on the initial pass. Since a single strike would rarely bring down such a large animal, a hunter would ride alongside as it fled, making repeated

Above: Apsaroke (or Crow) tribesmen armed with lances, a surprisingly versatile weapon that enabled a good horseman to thrust in any direction while remaining out of reach of his opponent.

thrusts until the prey collapsed. The use of the lance in combat was not very different.

Even en masse, Native American horsemen fought as warriors rather than formally trained cavalry, striking whatever targets presented themselves then riding clear of the fight. There was nothing to be gained from becoming embroiled in a melee; instead each horseman followed a doctrine sometimes described by modern fighter pilots as 'one pass and haul ass'.

The overall effect was bewildering for the target, with warriors racing by, making a strike and then disappearing while others dashed in from a different direction. Accompanied by archery or gunfire from horseback, this style of warfare played to the strengths of the individual warrior and expert horseman.

the spring a young girl was needed. The last known Morning Star ritual was in 1838.

The Pawnee were enemies of the Sioux and Cheyenne, and became natural allies of the US government in its wars against them. Pawnee scouts served with distinction in the Powder River Expedition of 1865 as well as wars against the Comanche and Sioux. In the meantime, warriors were employed as guards for the expanding railroads.

THE CHEYENNE

The Cheyenne migrated onto the Great Plains in the 1700s. Prior to this they undertook several migrations as a result of conflict with other tribes. In the 1600s, the Cheyenne lived in what is now Minnesota, where they encountered French traders in 1689. Conflict broke out with other tribes – notably the Sioux and the Chippewa – for control of this lucrative trade, and the Cheyenne were forced to move out of the area.

Above: Chiefs of the Cheyenne assembled for a Sun Dance, held at the beginning of summer or late in the spring.

In the early 1700s, the Cheyenne migrated to the valley of the Sheyenne River, a tributary of the Red River to the south of Lake Winnipeg. There they were a sedentary community, building semi-subterranean lodges as dwellings and relying primarily upon farming. Bison hunting began around this time, with parties sent out onto the plains to hunt then returning to the tribe's villages.

Contact with Europeans made horses available to the Cheyenne, who moved westwards to the Black Hills in the 1780s. There they became dependent on the bison, using horses to hunt over a wider area and living in tipis to allow the tribe to follow the herds. The Council of Forty-Four was founded around this time. Each of the 10 bands making up the Cheyenne nation provided four chiefs, with four more 'old man chiefs' selected for their wisdom and long service to the tribe.

The ability of Cheyenne hunters to range widely on their horses inevitably caused friction with other tribes who resented intrusions into their hunting grounds. The Cheyenne had an advantage in these conflicts,

The Horse in the New World

The horse is not native to the Americas, so before the arrival of Europeans all tribes hunted and fought on foot, walking or using canoes for transport. Those in the northeastern woodlands had relatively little incentive to adopt riding animals, but for the plains tribes the horse offered such enormous advantages in warfare and mobility that once some tribes had acquired horses their neighbours had to do the same.

The first were introduced to the Caribbean islands by Spanish expeditions, then into Mexico. Breeding began more or less as soon as the first settlements were established; livestock were permitted to wander as they pleased and would breed naturally. Wild herds began to appear, and the local tribes took advantage once the possibilities became apparent. By the mid-1600s, European settlers were bringing horses into the eastern coastal region and herds descended from the original Spanish arrivals had spread into northern Mexico and the southern Great Plains. By 1750, horses were available to tribes living in the northwest and had become integral to the Native American way of life.

Below: Leaders of six tribes in full regalia. Each feather in a headdress represented a respected action or a wise decision honoured by the tribe.

conferred not only by their possession of horses but also by guns bought from European traders. Although they had moved west the tribe did not lose contact with their European trading partners and benefited considerably from the association.

The Cheyenne fragmented into northern and southern tribes around 1825 as a result of internal disputes about trade. The northern Cheyenne moved to Montana and the southern to Oklahoma. Encroachment by white settlers was resisted by the tribe's four warrior societies, and after 1830 a fifth society, known as Dog Men but often called Dog Soldiers by outsiders, emerged. A sixth society – Crazy (or Foolish) Dogs – later emerged.

> ## *"Pemmican was produced by drying and shredding buffalo meat then mixing it with buffalo fat."*

Facing page: To the Sioux and other tribes of the Great Plains a good horse was a status symbol as well as an essential tool, to be casually shown off whenever appropriate.

Below: Pemmican was often flavoured with dried fruit or berries; here a Cheyenne woman prepares wild cherries using a stone mortar and pestle.

The military societies formed a counterpoint to the Council of Forty-Four in Cheyenne governance as well as a fighting force. Among their traditional enemies were the Apache, Comanche and Kiowa. The Dog Men eventually became a separate band within the tribe rather than a military society, largely due to an incident in which their leader Porcupine Bear intervened in a drunken fight between two of his cousins and killed one of them. He was outlawed for killing a fellow tribe member and for a time the Dog Men were forced to live apart from other Cheyenne.

The 1849 cholera epidemic severely depleted the Cheyenne nation, and the Dog Men gradually came to be viewed as a band within the tribe as they absorbed survivors of other groups. Although outlaws they led the fight against white encroachment and gradually lost their outlaw status.

THE SIOUX CONFEDERATION

The Sioux Confederation migrated westwards onto the Great Plains at the beginning of the 1800s, splitting into three allied tribes. These were the Lakota, the Dakota and the Nakota. Each tribe consisted of several bands, with the Lakota being the largest and most warlike. Their way of life once on the plains was similar to other nomadic tribes, with villages moving to follow the buffalo or to go to where other prey were plentiful.

Like some other tribes, the Sioux made pemmican as a way of preserving food for the winter or for use in long journeys. Pemmican was produced by drying and shredding buffalo meat then mixing it with buffalo fat. Additional ingredients such as dried fruit or berries might also be added. The pemmican hardened as it cooled, creating a preserved high-energy food that might keep for a year or more.

Pemmican was sought after by Europeans, notably the Hudson's Bay Company. The company

Firearms in the Early 19th Century

At the beginning of the 19th century, flintlock weapons were the best available. Double-barrelled firearms offered a second shot without reloading, but unless multiple weapons were available it was necessary to undergo a lengthy process to ready another shot. Experienced fighters took advantage of this, inducing their opponents to take a hasty shot then rushing in before reloading could be completed. It was not uncommon for the best shots in a group to be handed weapons loaded by others, enabling them to maintain a firing position and keep up a rapid rate of fire.

The development of cap-and-ball weapons greatly increased individual firepower. Rifle-muskets firing a minié ball were far more accurate and had a greater range than the preceding flintlocks, and their percussion cap-initiated mechanism was more reliable.

Such weapons were standard issue for infantry by the time of the Civil War, although some flintlocks were still in use and could be highly effective in skilled hands.

The cap-and-ball revolver represented an enormous leap forward. Five of its six cylinders could be pre-loaded – a lengthy process requiring sealing the chamber with grease – and the last left empty to avoid an accidental discharge. The tactic of drawing fire and then rushing in was suddenly a lot less viable, especially if the shooter had additional pre-loaded cylinders ready to be swapped into his revolver when it was empty.

Left: Little Wound and other chiefs of the Sioux nation. Little Wound fought the Pawnee at Massacre Canyon and later joined the Ghost Dance movement.

saw it as a useful alternative to transporting rations across the Atlantic Ocean, and bought sufficient quantities at its stations along the Red River that control of the pemmican trade was almost as important as a stake in the fur trade. For the Sioux and other plains tribes, however, pemmican was mainly important as a means to get through a tough winter.

The Sioux had many similarities with other plains tribes, but spoke

headdress were earned one by one for deeds of valour or wise acts that benefited the tribe, although a warrior's first feather might be given to him upon reaching adulthood. It was common to wear one or two feathers in battle, but the full headdress was only used on important occasions.

The bestowal of a feather was recognized as an occasion, similar to the presentation of medals in European cultures. A warrior might meditate and prepare himself for days before the presentation of his feather, which would be attached to a pole for display until he had enough

> ## *"The bestowal of a feather was recognized as an occasion, similar to the presentation of medals in European cultures."*

their own language and observed their own customs. Their clothing was generally similar to that of other tribes, with women wearing highly decorated dresses for ceremonial occasions. Decoration often symbolized the deeds of their family in war, the hunt or on other occasions where a tribe member won renown.

For men, a headdress of fur, beads and eagle feathers symbolized accomplishment. Other tribes adopted a similar practice with designs varying from one tribe to another, but it may be that the Sioux were the original creators. The feathers in a

to make a headdress. This was a solemn undertaking carried out by men only, with the warrior's friends taking part in the preparation.

The Sioux nation came into conflict with the US government in 1854 when soldiers entered an encampment to arrest a tribe member for stealing a cow. This was beyond their remit, as such issues were the responsibility of the Indian Agent assigned to the tribe. The officer in charge, Lieutenant Grattan, was recently commissioned and openly contemptuous of the tribes. It is widely believed that he was looking for a fight.

Above: The Grattan Massacre came about largely as a result of an inexperienced officer's desire for action, and triggered punitive action against the Sioux.

The tribe refused to allow the arrest to take place, correctly asserting that the military had no jurisdiction to carry it out and that it would instead be handled by the Indian Agent. Chief Conquering Bear tried to negotiate a peaceful settlement, offering to compensate the cow's owner from his own property. Negotiations broke down and one of the soldiers nervously opened fire, mortally wounding Conquering Bear.

> *"Negotiations broke down and one of the soldiers nervously opened fire, mortally wounding Conquering Bear."*

In what has since become known as the 'Grattan Massacre' or 'Grattan Affair', Grattan and some of his party were quickly killed. Red Cloud led a pursuit of the remaining soldiers, who were chased down and killed. The incident brought about the First Sioux War and, arguably, was a factor in later conflicts.

The First Sioux War took the form of a punitive expedition by US troops, beginning in August 1855. An attack on a Sioux village at Ash Hollow resulted in the massacre of Sioux women and children, after which the force moved on to seek other targets. Encountering none, it withdrew and for the next 10 years the Sioux did not resist the continued encroachment onto their lands. A treaty at Fort Laramie in 1868 established the Great Sioux Reservation, but when gold was found in the Black Hills this treaty ceased to be honoured.

THE SAND CREEK MASSACRE

In 1851 the United States government signed a treaty near Fort Laramie, Wyoming, with representatives of several major tribes including the Assiniboine, Arapaho, Cheyenne, Crow and Sioux. Under its terms, the US guaranteed the sovereignty of the tribes' lands and stated that it made no claims upon this territory but would make annual payments to the tribes in return for safe passage for settlers headed for Oregon and the far west. The treaty also established the terms for peace among the tribes.

The Fort Laramie Treaty was not a success. The annuities were not paid in many cases, and war broke out almost immediately between the Crow and an alliance of Cheyenne and Lakota. The discovery of gold in the region brought about an influx of settlers who were more interested in riches than the terms of a treaty. This was more than just territorial encroachment. The settlers' towns and mines depended upon local resources to feed their population, putting pressure on game and causing the tribes to go hungry. Incidents were inevitable, especially since the US government made little or no attempt to control the settlers.

In 1860 the US government offered a new treaty, under whose terms the tribes were required to surrender most of their lands. Some chiefs agreed to the terms of the treaty but the Cheyenne Council of Forty-Four and the Dog Men military society refused to recognize it. Taking advantage of forces raised for the Civil War, the governor of Colorado began destroying camps belonging to the Cheyenne and their allies. The situation escalated into open warfare when Cheyenne chiefs were shot while approaching Colorado troops in the hope of opening peaceful dialogue. Those members of the tribes not wishing to fight the US government were

Below: The Treaty of Fort Laramie was a real opportunity to resolve the tensions between tribes on the Great Plains and white settlers, but by this time there was simply too little trust remaining.

invited to place themselves under its protection at Big Sandy Creek for the duration of the war, but many – not without reason – mistrusted the offer.

Thus the encampment at Sand Creek contained mostly women, children and old men when US troops arrived in November 1864. Despite guarantees of safety and a flag of truce flying over the settlement, the US force attacked and carried out a deliberate massacre. Among the dead were many of the chiefs who had been opposed to war, whereas those who wanted to fight were elsewhere. The Cheyenne and their allied tribes responded with their own raids and massacres, and although an inquiry was provided

Below: The attack on Sand Creek was launched against noncombatants and pro-peace chiefs, ensuring the war would be longer and more savage than otherwise might have been the case.

with evidence of a needless slaughter of noncombatants, no charges were brought against any of the participants at Sandy Creek. Another treaty was offered in 1865, and once again within months it had been revised to vastly reduce the territory retained by the tribes.

JULESBURG AND THE PLATTE BRIDGE CAMPAIGN

The Cheyenne and their allies among the Lakota and Arapaho retaliated with raids against settlements in the region, notably what is now Julesburg in Colorado. At the time, this was a way station

on the westward wagon trail with a cavalry fort located nearby. Rather than assault the fort's defences, the Cheyenne launched a small attack then quickly fled, drawing the cavalry after them. The intent was to draw the garrison into an ambush outside the fort, and it was very nearly a success.

Alerted by firing from over-eager members of the ambush party, the cavalry force was not in the killing zone when the attack began. Instead it was pursued back towards the fort. Some of the cavalrymen were caught and overwhelmed, while the rest managed to enter the fort and take up defensive positions. Unable to sortie against the greatly superior Native American force, the cavalry and the civilians who had fled to the fort were forced to watch the way station looted and destroyed.

Stung by this defeat, the US military launched a punitive expedition. This was a complete failure, finding only a camp that had been recently vacated, and

with casualties from frostbite the force withdrew. The targets of the raid had begun a move to the Black Hills and the Powder River region, although they used their mobility to strike at targets over a wide area. These included settlements, isolated ranches and stagecoach stations as well as herds from which several hundred head of cattle were stolen.

Above: Warriors of the Dakota, part of the Sioux Confederacy. Chasing a warband of this sort was always dangerous; their leaders were adept at leading pursuers into an ambush.

> *"Some of the cavalrymen were caught and overwhelmed, while the rest managed to enter the fort and take up defensive positions."*

While the nations were on the march they took the opportunity to raid Julesburg a second time, with the cavalry detachment there unable to do more than shelter in their fort. In July 1865 the tribes made a raid in force involving around

Native American Command and Control

Above: Displays of riding prowess and horseback tricks encouraged warriors to hone their skills as they sought to outdo one another and impress onlookers.

The forces fielded by the tribes were composed of bands of warriors rather than organized forces of soldiers. A group of warriors followed whatever leader it chose and members were free to depart or join another band if their leader took actions they disapproved of. Thus a force was composed of bands-of-bands, with particularly charismatic leaders directing the actions of large numbers of warriors. These charismatic leaders had earned the respect of their followers by exploit and reputation, but that did not necessarily translate to a gift for strategy. Holding a large force together for any length of time was

virtually impossible, and imposing military discipline was equally difficult. At times, experienced warriors belonging to the Dog Men society were able to keep the more unruly elements of a force in line, but often a well-planned ambush or coordinated attack was derailed by a few hotheads seeking glory or plunder.

Parts of a force on the move might detach themselves to go hunting or raiding, or to return home if they had captured horses or other loot that seemed sufficient. As a result, campaigns tended to fizzle out either because they were not very successful or because they

were successful enough to satisfy the warriors' desire for horses and glory.

Those with a serious grudge against their enemies or who were members of a military society – or highly loyal to a particular chief – might be persuaded to stay the course, but for the most part a large campaign was a short-lived affair of cooperative action rather than a concerted effort.

This lack of formal organization made it just as difficult to make peace as war – at any given time some groups would want peace but others were dead set on raiding for profit or to avenge an attack made upon their people.

1000 warriors. The campaign struck several targets, including the Platte River crossings and way stations on the surrounding trails. The heavily outnumbered defenders were unable to do more than hold their fortified positions, allowing the raiders to take large numbers of animals and burn buildings outside the defended perimeter. Those that were lured out to chase raiding parties ran into ambushes and were lucky to be able to withdraw.

The US response was poorly handled. Expeditionary forces failed to find their targets or tired their mounts out so badly they had to return to base. An attempt to move a band of Lakota away from Fort Laramie resulted in them joining the conflict against the US. Similarly, the defence of the Platte crossings was confused and rather limp, although the bridge was not taken or destroyed. Ultimately the attack failed due to internal disputes among the Native American contingents rather than the efforts of the defenders.

THE POWDER RIVER EXPEDITION

Launched in July 1865, the Powder River Expedition was a punitive operation launched in retaliation for the Platte River and Julesburg attacks. The strategy was typical of 'colonial' warfare undertaken by European powers in the same era; it was not possible to deploy

"The US response was poorly handled. Expeditionary forces failed to find their targets or tired their mounts out..."

enough troops to hold down an area, so key points were defended and attacks discouraged by punitive raids. This mode of warfare was not dissimilar to that used by the Native American tribes, who could not maintain large forces in the field for any length of time.

Below: Although the force assembled for the Powder River Expedition was formidable, its supply 'tail' made it slow-moving and vulnerable to attack by more mobile forces.

The expedition aimed to set up a fort for use as a base and to help control the area once the main force withdrew. It took the form of three parallel columns advancing towards the projected fort site. Its orders were unequivocal –

> "Even without the constant threat of attack, the advance was a struggle for the US force, suffering from lack of provisions and poor morale..."

no peace was to be agreed and captured warriors were to be executed. Some officers tried to oppose these orders, and in any case they were not always obeyed in the field, but the intent was clear.

The campaign opened with skirmishes during the advance, in which both sides achieved minor

Below: Hook Nose was a leader of the heroic sort rather than a strategist. His favoured tactic was to personally draw enemy fire away from his warriors, trusting in his extremely strong medicine to protect him.

successes. One group of supply wagons was trapped and unable to move for several days until a relief force arrived to drive off the surrounding Native Americans. Even without the constant threat of attack, the advance was a struggle for the US force, suffering from lack of provisions and poor morale among dispirited soldiers, and this situation was made much worse by the harassing tactics of the tribes. Nevertheless, the columns moved towards a rendezvous near the Black Hills. By the beginning of September 1865 one column was camped at Alkali Creek. This formidable force was more or less immune to direct attack, but proved susceptible to the usual Native American tactics of drawing out elements and then defeating them.

A raid to steal horses served the dual purpose of drawing an intervention and satisfying the warriors' desire to have something to show for their efforts. The small force that tried to respond was ambushed, as were hunting parties over the next few days. The US force was short of food at this point and was beginning to find its position untenable. It resumed its march in the hope of making a junction with the main column and obtaining supplies, and was harassed en route.

The US columns were unsure of one another's location, a problem that was made worse by attacks on scouting parties. They were forced to take a best guess and march on, hoping to run into friendly forces or at least signs of their passage. This groping about in hostile territory brought one column close to a village of Arapaho, Cheyenne

Armour

In colder weather the plains tribes wore buckskin clothing that offered at least a degree of protection against weapons, but little in the way of deliberately created armour was used. The exception was a breastplate of bone, formed into hair-pipes and threaded onto thongs. The breastplate was tied in place behind the neck and around the back.

It is questionable how much protection this armour actually provided. Projectiles such as arrows and bullets would easily penetrate it but a poorly executed strike from a hand weapon might be turned aside, and any protection is better than none. The main benefit of the breastplate was spiritual and perhaps psychological – the warrior felt protected and was therefore emboldened in battle.

Armour of this sort had important ceremonial functions, and was often decorated with feathers or other tokens. The ceremonial aspect also added to the armour's protective qualities – at least for those brought up in Native American culture – as it provided what might be termed magical protection to the wearer that far outweighed its physical capabilities.

Left: The bone breastplate was a highly decorative item and the hallmark of a warrior, regardless of how much physical protection it provided.

The Bozeman Trail

The discovery of gold in what is now Colorado triggered the Pike's Peak gold rush, which was followed by a surge northwards as new and more promising deposits were located. In the early 1860s, prospectors flocked to Montana Territory. Among them was John Bozeman, who quickly realized that the real money was to be made from the miners rather than being one of them. He decided to set up an easier and quicker route to the new goldfields from the Oregon Trail, and against the advice of local 'mountain men' he chose a route straight through the lands of the Sioux.

Geographically this was a good route, as it avoided rough terrain and provided good grazing for animals along the Powder River. However, this was prime hunting land for the same reason, and it had been guaranteed to the Sioux in the 1851 treaty of Fort Laramie. As Bozeman led the first party along his new route they were confronted by warriors who warned them to turn back. Most did, but Bozeman and a handful of others slipped through and demonstrated the practicability of the route. Wagon trains began using the trail in 1864, generally without serious opposition. Forts were built to protect the wagon trains and herds moving along the trail, which caused great resentment among the local tribes. The increased tensions helped set in motion the Julesburg and Platte Bridge attacks.

Below: The Bozeman Trail was a major cause of conflict with the tribes whose lands it crossed. John Bozeman eventually met his end on the trail.

and Sioux, whose warriors launched an attack. This developed into a set-piece battle in which the Cheyenne leader Hook Nose (also known as Roman Nose) rode up and down in front of the enemy taunting them until his horse was finally shot from under him.

This was a tactic Hook Nose favoured, causing the enemy to waste their ammunition while sapping their morale with his apparent invulnerability. This he ascribed to his careful preparations for battle in which he diligently prepared his spirit and his medicine to thwart the enemy. Although he lost a horse on this occasion, Hook Nose survived the incident.

Under fire from artillery, the Native American attack eventually dissipated and the warriors pulled back into the woods along the Powder River. They remained close to the column and continued to harass it as it moved slowly along the river. Eventually, the column was located by scouts and directed to Fort Connor, which had been established by other forces. Exhausted and hungry, the force that arrived at Fort Connor was militarily useless and could undertake no further operations. The goal of establishing a fort was accomplished, but beyond this the expedition had achieved nothing beyond providing the tribes of the region with a target.

These harassment tactics were adopted out of necessity – there were too many rifles and artillery pieces in the columns for a head-on attack to be successful – but they were effective. The shadowing

Above: The archetypical image of a wagon train attacked by Native American warriors is more a product of popular fiction than reality, though attacks certainly did occur from time to time.

Native American force could choose when to attack and when to stay out of range, shooting from positions of cover that the wagon column had to pass close by. The

> *"Native American warriors always had the option to withdraw from a losing fight, but the US force never did."*

Native American warriors always had the option to withdraw from a losing fight, but the US force never did. The harassment was thus not only a matter of causing casualties and denying the column the ability to forage for food, it was a powerful psychological gambit as well. The tactic was a partial success in this case – the Powder River Expedition was defeated in the tactical sense but achieved its strategic goal of building a fort on the Bozeman Trail.

Below: Chief Little Crow of the Dakota people adopted many European customs and manner of dress, but ultimately took up arms to lead his people in the Dakota War of 1862.

THE DAKOTA WAR

Part of the Sioux Confederation, the Dakota agreed a treaty in 1851 under whose terms they were granted a reservation on the Minnesota River, ceding their lands in return for regular payments from the government. These were late or not made at all, and much of the money was embezzled by agents of the Office of Indian Affairs. By 1862 the Dakota were suffering great hardship and could not feed their people from the resources of their small reservation. Nor could they buy what they needed, as the promised payments from the government were again missing or late. By the time the money arrived, conflict had begun.

There was probably no intent to start a war on the part of the tribe's leaders, but when a hunting party killed a group of white settlers retaliation became inevitable. The Dakota decided not to wait for the troops to arrive, but instead launched a campaign against local settlements. The Dakota chief Little Crow wrote to the authorities explaining why his tribe had gone on the warpath, citing the uncaring and contemptuous attitude of local traders who refused to let the tribe have desperately needed food on credit.

Among the first to be killed in the raids was one of the traders, who had made inflammatory comments to the effect that the tribe should eat grass if they were so hungry. His body was found with a mouthful of grass. Raids on several settlements ensued, forcing the population to flee the area. An initial response by a company of infantry was ambushed at the Minnesota River and defeated in the Battle of Redwood Ferry.

Bypassing Fort Ridgely, the Dakota attacked New Ulm and partially burned down the town, although the defenders were able to hold out in an improvised defensive position. Once reinforcements reached the town the Dakota broke off and attacked Fort Ridgely instead. They could not penetrate the defences, but their attack tied down US forces that were thus unavailable for offensive operations or to reinforce threatened areas. This enabled the Dakota to overrun several small outposts such as stagecoach stations and small settlements with little resistance.

The US response was slow in coming, largely due to the ongoing Civil War. Eventually a force under General John Pope was assembled to fight the Dakota if negotiations failed. Little Crow was willing to negotiate and outlined the reasons for the war, but the US wanted unconditional surrender. The newly raised US force, short of supplies and

Below: After an initial skirmish on 19th August, the battle of New Ulm began in earnest on the 23rd. Over 600 Dakota warriors took part.

Facing page: Chief Little Crow in European dress. His given name, Thaóyate Dúta, translates as 'His Red Nation'.

weapons, made slow progress and had a tendency to straggle on the march, presenting an ideal target for an attack.

The intended ambush was triggered early by an advance party foraging for food, bringing about an encounter battle rather than an ambush. The decisive factor was the experience of some of the US troops. While some units were filled with new recruits, the 3rd Minnesota Volunteer Infantry was a veteran formation whose troops led the fight and gained enough

time for their inexperienced comrades to get organized. The conflict, which became known as the Battle of Wood Lake, ended with victory for the US forces. Little Crow's prestige was diminished, and less warlike chiefs pushed for peace.

The prospect of more casualties made continued warfare unpalatable and large segments of the Dakota surrendered. They were eventually joined by the rest of the tribe, which was forced to relocate westwards.

Cartridge Firearms

Above: The percussion-cap mechanism of the Sharps Rifle permitted a greater rate of fire and much easier loading on horseback than preceding weapons, although not to the same extent as unitary cartridge firearms.

The first unitary cartridges were produced in the early 1800s, but it was some time before weapons that used them became widely available. Indeed, obtaining a weapon that required specific pre-produced ammunition was not always desirable for those living far from industrial centres. Powder and percussion caps were universal, so only the ball or bullet needed to be specific to a user's weapon. Once he armed himself with a firearm using unitary cartridges that changed.

However, the ability to load and fire one quickly, and the greater uniformity of charges that in turn enhanced precision, offered many advantages. Warriors equipped

with single-shot breechloaders could outshoot those equipped with flintlock weapons, and could reload on horseback. Repeating firearms took this even further. A rifleman could shoot as fast as he could work the bolt or lever of his weapon, and he could load several rounds in the time it took to reload a rifle-musket.

The earliest pump-action shotguns appeared in the mid-19th century, and by the end of the century early semi-automatic weapons were becoming available. Mechanically operated weapons such as the Gatling gun were also available in the mid-1800s, although the first true machine guns did not see action until the 1890s.

Earlier weapons remained in use long after unitary cartridge firearms became available. Single-shot rifles were entirely adequate for a hunter or, if taken to war, by a warrior who could take an aimed shot from cover then disappear while he reloaded.

Likewise, bows and spears remained viable weapons in the hands of those who knew how to use them. However, the Native American tribes saw the value of advanced weaponry and obtained it whenever they could. On occasion they outgunned the US troops sent against them, since the latter were often still equipped with weapons left over from the Civil War.

Coup Sticks

'Counting coup' was an act of skill and bravado in which a warrior would touch but not harm an enemy. This might be done with a weapon, but the achievement was greater if the warrior used either his hand or a 'coup stick' upon which notches were cut to indicate successful strikes. Coup was also counted for feats such as stealing horses or touching an enemy's home or fortifications.

Getting close enough to strike any blow was dangerous, and a warrior who chose not to put his enemy out of action took even greater risks. Touching the enemy then escaping without being wounded was considered more of an achievement than being injured in the attempt, although the deed was still respected. This display of courage and skill might be rewarded with eagle feathers, which were attached to the stick itself or to a headdress. Other coup tokens included scalps, beads and decoration added to clothing.

Counting coup was not just about personal status. An enemy who had been touched but not harmed might realize he had received a demonstration of both capability and restraint, and might be induced to talk rather than fight on. Counting coup was also used as a training method, with warriors keeping score against one another in non-lethal fights. Those who were thought to be dishonest about admitting they had been touched risked being struck for real.

RED CLOUD'S WAR

After the near-fiasco of the Powder River Expedition, the US government tried to impose a treaty that would guarantee the safety of those using the Bozeman Trail. A force of around 700 government troops was moved into the area at the same time. Red Cloud, a chief of the Oglala Lakota, was not willing to be strongarmed into a treaty, and decided to fight.

The US forces deployed in the area were reasonably secure in their forts, at least in the short term. However, in December 1866, Captain William Fetterman sortied out from Fort Phil Kearny with 80 men against the orders of his superior. None made it back alive, and the action became known as the Fetterman Massacre or Fetterman Fight. A request for assistance from Fort Laramie brought a relief column in mid-January, but plans for a major punitive expedition soon came to nothing.

Hostilities continued in 1867 with an attack on a woodcutting party whose escort turned out to be armed with breechloading rifles, giving them a firepower advantage over their opponents. Fighting from a hasty fortification thrown together from wagons and boxes, the woodcutters and their escorting troops successfully defended themselves. Their estimate of hundreds of Native American casualties was probably inflated; the tribes later stated they lost six warriors in the action, which became known as the Wagon Box Fight.

Facing page: Red Cloud was a highly respected warrior who had distinguished himself in wars against the Pawnee and other tribes, counting coup no less than 80 times.

"Red Cloud, a chief of the Oglala Lakota, was not willing to be strongarmed into a treaty, and decided to fight."

Above: The Fetterman Massacre followed a familiar pattern; an over-confident leader placed his force where it could be overwhelmed, and his troops paid the price.

Facing page: 'Plenty Coups' was a pidgin translation of Alaxchiiaahush, meaning 'many war achievements' – a name not lightly bestowed.

Skirmishing went on until 1868, when a new treaty at Fort Laramie guaranteed the lands north of the Platte to the tribes. The Bozeman Trail forts were abandoned, after which the tribes burned them down. Thus Red Cloud's War ended as a victory for the Native Americans, although the region would see renewed conflict in the coming years.

THE CROW

The Crow migrated to the Great Plains from the northeastern woodland region, probably near Lake Erie and the upper Mississippi. They were gradually pushed west, notably by the Sioux. Although the Crow were related to the Sioux, at least linguistically, they were frequently enemies. Eventually the Crow settled around the Yellowstone River and adopted a nomadic lifestyle typical of the area.

The Crow traded horses to other tribes and used their own to undertake trading expeditions. They were not hostile to the white settlers, and sided with the US government against their traditional enemies the Sioux. This was encouraged by their chief Plenty Coups, who had a vision as a young man that suggested the white man would come to dominate the land, and those tribes that resisted would be destroyed.

Plenty Coups encouraged cooperation with the US government, and although his tribe had to accept a reservation like others, they were granted their current homeland. Crow warriors served as scouts for the

Left: Plenty Coups made several visits to the White House on behalf of his people, and was able to secure the future of his people on their ancestral lands.

Facing page: Without the assistance of Crow scouts such as this one, it is arguable that the US military would have fared far worse in its campaigns against the Great Plains tribes.

US Army and upon occasion saved government troops from disaster. A small party of Crow scouts witnessed the disaster at Little Big Horn and subsequently reported the events to the authorities.

Plenty Coups got his name from his achievements in war. To become a chief, a Crow warrior had to perform four specific feats: leading a war party that succeeded without any casualties; stealing a horse from the enemy; touching an enemy with a coup stick during a fight; and taking a weapon away from a resisting opponent. Plenty Coups did all this and more as a young man, becoming a chief in 1876. In his later career he repeatedly visited Washington on behalf of his people, and represented the Native American nations at the dedication of the Tomb of the Unknown Soldier. His coup stick and war bonnet remain on display there.

THE BLACK HILLS WAR

In 1874 an expedition led by George Armstrong Custer was sent to the Black Hills to find a suitable location for a fort and to search for gold. There is some debate about how rich the gold veins were, but the discovery of deposits sparked a rush in which prospectors and

---

"…the discovery of deposits sparked a rush in which prospectors and miners ignored the treaties their government had made."

---

miners ignored the treaties their government had made. The US authorities tried to prevent the encroachment on Native American lands, but with little success, and the endeavour was soon abandoned. The government then attempted to buy the gold-bearing land. These were among the few parts of the reservation valued by the inhabitants, who naturally refused to sell.

A party of chiefs including Red Cloud met with US government officials in Washington, citing previous treaties and guarantees. The government countered with another offer to buy their land, under the terms of a deal whereby the tribes would relocate to Oklahoma. The delegation would have none of it, at least in part because previous treaties had not been honoured. They returned to

The Sun Dance and the Vision Quest

The Sun Dance was performed with some variations by many plains tribes. It took place early in the year when the hunting was good, partly to celebrate the passing of winter and the coming of more plentiful times and partly to take advantage of sufficient game to support a large gathering.

The Sun Dance, even in its mildest form, was a difficult and exhausting undertaking in which the subject would dance intermittently over a period of several days, fasting in between. Sometimes the dance was accompanied by additional suffering inflicted by thin rods piercing the skin, to which a heavy ritual object was attached.

The main Sun Dance ritual was accompanied by less significant ceremonies that were undertaken by a greater number of participants. The practice was outlawed by the US government in 1883 although it was still practised, and over time a more moderate form of the traditional ceremony emerged.

The Vision Quest was another important ritual. It was part of the Sun Dance tradition but also undertaken separately. The subject was required to prepare himself then go to an isolated place, where he would fast and use hallucinogenic herbs. If successful, the quest would result in contact with a spirit guardian and a dream that would be interpreted by the tribe's medicine men. Visions were important to the strategic choices made by great leaders such as Sitting Bull.

Below: A Cheyenne Sun Dance. The ceremony was prohibited in Canada until the 1950s and in the USA until the 1970s.

their tribes empty-handed, and the US government began to explore other options.

Attempts to prevent encroachment on the reservations were suspended, and orders were given for all Native Americans to return to their reservation. This was not possible due to the onset of winter, and non-compliance was then used as a pretext for a punitive campaign. This began with a cavalry raid under the command of Colonel Joseph Reynolds on a camp of the Cheyenne on the Powder River, who were not hostile and caught by surprise.

The population were ushered to safety by their warriors, who then began a counterattack. Although the settlement was burned and hundreds of horses captured by the cavalry, resistance continued in the form of rifle fire from nearby bluffs.

Above: Crow scout Bloody Knife accompanied George Armstrong Custer on the 1874 Black Hills Expedition, which discovered gold in the region.

"Others were pushed into the war camp by the fact that the US had attacked a settlement that was not hostile."

Below: Colonel Joseph Reynolds was suspended from the army by a court-martial for his handling of the 1876 expedition, and subsequently resigned his commission.

The cavalry withdrew but failed to find their supporting force and the supplies it carried until the following day. In the meantime, most of the captured horses were retrieved by a Cheyenne raiding party. The tribe was impoverished by the raid, but suffered very

few casualties. The impression gained of the US forces was that they were ineffectual, which encouraged those who wanted to fight. Others were pushed into the war camp by the fact that the US had attacked a settlement that was not hostile. This was not the first time government forces had been careless about target identification; indeed, many felt that 'the only good Indian was a dead Indian' and disregarded concerns such as which tribes were friendly or even allied to the government against their enemies.

EXPEDITION

Thus began the Black Hills War, otherwise known as the Great Sioux War. A few weeks later, in June 1876, a new and much larger expedition was launched. This took the form of three parallel columns that were to converge and bring the Sioux to battle. The columns advanced along a similar path to previous expeditions, most of which had ended badly for the government forces.

Fully aware of what was unfolding, the Sioux war chief Crazy Horse declared that he would attack if the US force crossed the Tongue River, and he duly did. Crazy Horse was an experienced warrior in his mid-thirties, by all accounts a quiet and rather strange man when not on the warpath, but he was well respected. He had seen action at the Platte River crossings and the Fetterman Fight. His preferred tactic was long-range sniping, giving the large US force no clear target to attack. He then pulled his force back.

Crazy Horse may have hoped that he had made his point without too much bloodshed, and that the US force might withdraw. Instead the column began to advance, reinforced by scouts from the Crow and Shoshone tribes who were long-time enemies of the Sioux and quite happy to fight them. Hoping to benefit from greater mobility the US commander left his supply wagons behind under guard and made a rapid advance towards the Rosebud Creek, where he expected to find a Sioux village.

What might have been a stealthy approach march was undone by Crow scouts shooting buffalo they encountered, and on the morning of 17 June 1876 the scouts came under fire from Sioux warriors positioned on high ground. The US column, curiously lax for a force deep in hostile territory, did not respond as the commanders thought this was just more buffalo hunting.

Crazy Horse and his warriors drove back the Crow and Shoshone scouts, and advanced rapidly on the disorganized US camp. Disaster was only prevented by the spirited resistance of the outnumbered scouts, and a confused and chaotic action unfolded. Crazy Horse directed his warriors to make hit-and-run attacks, perhaps hoping to trigger an unwise pursuit into an ambush. The US forces did not (or perhaps could not) take the bait, but this ensured the raiding parties could withdraw and regroup safely.

Assisted by a cavalry charge, the US force managed to make its way to higher ground and establish a defensive perimeter. The Sioux

Below: Although the Great Sioux War of 1876 did involve some close-quarters fighting, engagements of the sort depicted here were far less common than exchanges of rifle fire from cover.

Above: The Battle of the Rosebud was a defeat for the ineptly handled US forces, even though they gained control of the battleground. The Sioux achieved their aim of neutralizing the advance, then moved off.

Facing page: Sitting Bull's confidence in his own ability as a war leader was enhanced by a vision of soldiers falling upside-down into his camp, signifying a great defeat for the US forces.

warriors melted away in the face of successive charges by the US cavalry, but simply reformed and came back to the fight. The US force could therefore take and even hold ground but it was failing to defeat its enemy.

Incorrectly assuming that a threat to a nearby village would give the Sioux pause, a detachment of cavalry was sent out. In fact there was no village, and this action merely diluted the US force. Other elements were drawn out of their positions and heavily attacked. Again, the Shoshone and Crow scouts came to the rescue, and under the covering fire of infantry rifles the advanced force was able to rejoin the main body.

The Sioux and their allies eventually broke off after an unusually protracted fight. The US commander claimed victory in the usual sense – his force had possession of the battleground – but in reality his advance had been halted and his force remained in place for several weeks, playing little further part in the campaign. In the strategic sense, Crazy Horse had won a clear victory.

THE BATTLE OF LITTLE BIGHORN

Encouraged by their victories, the Sioux and Cheyenne continued to resist encroachment by settlers, gold miners and railroad builders. Chief Sitting Bull is credited with leadership of the Sioux nation during this period, although it is debatable whether he was formally in charge of a traditionally decentralized confederation. He had proven himself an adept war leader in earlier campaigns, and was adamant that he was not going to sell any land to the government. In 1875 he had a vision of a great victory and was confident that his nation could win the coming war. He recruited warriors from his own people and any others who would fight, and sheltered those who had suffered in raids against their villages.

As a result, Sitting Bull's encampment was already very large when he was joined by Crazy Horse and his men fresh from their victory at the Rosebud Creek on 17 June. As they camped on the banks of the Little Bighorn River, word came to the chiefs that another US

SITTING BULL.

Copyrighted by D. F. Barry, 1885,
BISMARCK, DAK.

D. F. BARRY,   BISMARCK, DAKOTA.

Right: 'Custer's Last Stand' was portrayed as a heroic sacrifice. In reality, he put his force in an untenable position out of arrogance and willfulness, and his soldiers paid the price.

cavalry force was approaching. This was commanded by Lieutenant-Colonel George Armstrong Custer, a self-promoting glory-hound who was hoping to rekindle his fame with a great victory. Custer's force was part of a column commanded by General Terry. Another, commanded by Colonel Gibbon, was headed for the Yellowstone River while General Crook's force had been stopped in its tracks by Crazy Horse on the Powder River. Although he was under orders to wait for the infantry, Custer pushed ahead and sighted the Sioux encampment. Grossly underestimating the force ranged against him, he resolved to attack.

Custer's force contained 12 companies of the 7th Cavalry, mostly veterans. He left a company to guard the pack train and split his force into three segments to attack from different directions. Captain Benteen was ordered to prevent the escape of the Sioux – an indication of how badly misjudged the action was – while Major Reno was to attack the southern side of the encampment with 175 men. Reno's force was quickly repulsed; they made a fighting withdrawal on to high ground, where they were attacked by large numbers of Cheyenne and Sioux warriors.

Custer's command of 210 men attacked from the north and was easily repulsed. As they fell back to higher ground, Crazy Horse led an enveloping movement that trapped

Facing page: Sitting Bull enjoyed a special status in Buffalo Bill's Wild West Show, since his mere presence was a huge draw. The show contributed to many myths of the 'Wild West'.

the cavalrymen. Shooting their horses to create a bulwark, Custer's men fought back as best they could but were overwhelmed by superior firepower and numbers. It is notable that the 7th Cavalry were armed with the Springfield Model 1873 'trapdoor' carbine, whose copper ammunition tended to expand in a hot gun and jam it.

Many Native American warriors had repeating rifles, outgunnng the cavalry's breechloaders even when they did work properly.

The detachments under Benteen and Reno were able to escape, and the Sioux moved off when the main US columns approached. In the meantime, Custer's command was wiped

Shooting from Horseback

Shooting from horseback, whether with a firearm or a bow, is a difficult business. The motion of the horse is not always predictable and makes careful use of sights problematic. With firearms, the solution is to aim generally along the top surface of the weapon rather than trying to focus on sights that are bouncing around. There is also the problem of pointing the weapon in the right direction. This can involve some awkward twisting around, which is made more difficult by a lack of stirrups.

The most important factor is not skill as a shooter, but as a rider. A bad shot on foot will still be a bad shot on horseback – probably worse – but a skilled marksman who cannot ride well will not hit anything from the saddle. Likewise, the horse is important. A mount used to working with a particular rider and willing to cooperate with him, or a trained cavalry mount accustomed to standard movements, provides a better shooting platform than a skittish or inexperienced horse.

A Native American warrior would learn to hunt from the saddle using a bow or rifle, guiding his mount

Shooting accurately from horseback, at speed and without stirrups, required close cooperation between the warrior and his mount. Those without the requisite skills would fail in the hunt or be defeated in war.

with his legs and timing his shots to avoid disruption by the horse's gait. Shots were taken at relatively short range using an instinctive point-and-shoot technique to lead the target and compensate for the

movement of the shooter. Such skills were a matter of necessity as well as pride – ammunition was expensive and sometimes hard to come by – and served equally well in war as in the hunt.

D. F. BARRY.

WEST SUPERIOR,

WIS.

SITTING BULL AND BUFFALO BILL.

Copyrighted 1897.

Above: The deliberate massacre of buffalo was carried out on an almost industrial scale, with hunter-tourists coming to the Great Plains to take part in what they presumably thought was great sport.

out, repeating a folly so many previous commanders had come to regret. In most cases, the troops had to be drawn into an ambush; Custer differed mainly in that he willingly put his force where it could be massacred.

Although Little Bighorn was a major victory, the strategic situation was still dire. The great encampment had to break up in order to find game, leaving the Sioux force depleted, but even so the US columns under Crook and Terry hesitated for some time, awaiting reinforcements. When they finally advanced, their numbers were too great for the Sioux and Cheyenne to resist. Skirmishes continued but there were no more great victories, and in May 1877 Crazy Horse surrendered to save his people from starvation. He was killed while imprisoned in Robinson.

Sitting Bull crossed into Canada, but his people suffered great hardship and eventually surrendered to the US government. Sitting Bull himself performed in Buffalo Bill's Wild West Show from 1885, and was killed in 1890. Concerns that he might be a figurehead for the Ghost Dance movement prompted orders for his imprisonment, and he was shot during a confused attempt to make an arrest.

BUFFALO EXTINCTION AND THE GHOST DANCE MOVEMENT

In order to ensure the Native Americans were confined to their reservations and had to take up farming, the US government actively encouraged the over-hunting of buffalo. Many were killed to feed railroad workers or expanding towns, but in many cases the herds were shot en masse and their carcasses left where they fell. Buffalo hunting became something of a fad, with rich Europeans and American city folk travelling west to take part in what amounted to massacres.

Within a few years, the buffalo was all but extinct on the Great Plains, and with it went the way of life of the people who lived there. Without herds to follow and hunt, the tribes were dependent on assistance from the US government, which forced them to remain on their reservations and could be used to apply influence. The plains warrior was not defeated by superior fighting prowess or firepower, but was forced to change his way of life in order to survive in

an altered environment. The battle of Little Bighorn is often called Custer's Last Stand, but in many ways it was the last hurrah of the plains tribes as well.

"Within a few years, the buffalo was all but extinct on the Great Plains, and with it went the way of life of the people who lived there."

Although the war was essentially won by the end of the 1880s, the possibility of further Native American resistance was taken seriously by the US

Below: The arrest of Chief Sitting Bull led to a tense situation that erupted into an exchange of gunfire, leaving Sitting Bull and 12 others dead.

government. The Ghost Dance movement of 1890 caused grave unease as a result. A variation on traditional dances, the Ghost Dance could, if performed correctly, make the white settlers go away and restore the tribal nations. It could even bring back the dead. While the US authorities are unlikely to have believed they were in danger of being danced out of existence, they considered the movement a possible rallying point for resistance and therefore took steps to suppress it.

The dance was outlawed, and when Sitting Bull – who was at the time living at Standing Rock – did

nothing to stop it being performed, orders were given for his arrest. His death in the ensuing scuffle sparked the Ghost Dance War – a series of skirmishes leading to the massacre at Wounded Knee. The latter came about when US troops tried to disarm a Lakota band camped at Wounded Knee Creek.

A young warrior resisted, and according to some accounts he accidentally discharged his weapon during the fracas. In response the troops fired back, and the Lakota warriors tried to take back their weapons to defend themselves. The whole affair was taking place under the guns of an

Below: The massacre at Wounded Knee came about partially out of fear of the Native American warriors' prowess. Nervous soldiers over-reacted with indiscriminate firepower and artillery fire.

Wealth, Generosity and Value

Horses became something of a status symbol among the tribes of the Great Plains, with possession of a particularly fine animal or several good horses a sign of wealth. However, wealth was not valued for its own sake. A warrior could make use of only so many mounts, and having too many did not impress others. Instead, wealth represented an ability to protect and support the family and tribe, to accomplish whatever needed doing and to be generous. The wealth of a warrior was measured not so much in terms of how many horses he possessed for his own use, but as his ability to give a horse to a worthy or needy friend. This tied in with the general conception that wealth was valuable as the capability to give rather than to keep.

A warrior was rich if he had much to give away and would do so when appropriate. One who had much and merely kept it was not wealthy in the same sense. Records exist of horses and guns traded by the northern tribes for 50 beaver pelts each, suggesting a roughly equal value. In practice, perceived value varied considerably and traders would bargain for whatever they could get.

The gift of a horse was thus a very significant matter, yet the wealthy warrior who made the gift might consider himself enriched by the act. He had parted with a material thing that he did not really need, and gained in return the respect and goodwill of his fellows.

artillery battery, which was turned on the encampment. Dozens of noncombatants and several US soldiers were killed by their fire.

The day after Wounded Knee, 30 December 1890, a final action took place between the Lakota and the US cavalry. Elements of the US 7th Cavalry were engaged

> *"…the Ghost Dance could, if performed correctly, make the white settlers go away and restore the tribal nations."*

by a force of Lakota warriors and had to be rescued by the 9th Cavalry. This action, known as the Drexel Mission Fight, was the last of the 'Indian Wars', although the far more notorious Wounded Knee massacre is more commonly considered the end point.

Tribes of the Southwest

The southwest is characterized by a dry climate with areas of desert and rocky terrain that makes long-distance movement difficult. These natural barriers helped isolate the cultures of the region from other Native American groups and, later, from European expansion westward. The difficulty of living on the Great Plains before the introduction of the horse restricted the eastwards drift, although early people of the Clovis and similar cultures did eventually make their way across the plains toward the Mississippi Valley and the northeastern woodlands.

The same difficulties limited contact with the cultures that arose to the east, ensuring that the tribes of the southwest went their own way until the horse enabled greater travel and the activities of Europeans pushed tribes towards the southwest. By this time distinct cultural differences existed and the sharing – or clash – of ideas produced further changes.

FROM MAMMOTH HUNTERS TO HORSEMEN

Around 9000 years ago the 'Cochise' culture emerged in what is now Arizona and New Mexico. It is named after Lake Cochise, which has since dried up to become a desert basin. The Cochise culture departed from that of the Clovis people in that foraging for plant-based foods was far more important than hunting. From around 6000 years ago hunting seems to have become more important, but at the same time the cultivation of maize began.

The Cochise culture was supplanted by three distinct cultural groups – the Ancestral Pueblo (also called Anasazi), Mogollon and Hohokam people. All three relied extensively upon agriculture, although their approaches varied. All three declined due to a prolonged period

Left: The stereotypical image of the Apache as rifle-armed horsemen has a basis in reality, but represents a short period in the history of the southwestern tribes.

Right: The largest 'great house' of the Ancestral Pueblo people, Pueblo Bonito contains around 800 rooms. It was constructed in stages over three centuries from 850 CE onward.

Below: This Jornada Mogollon petroglyph depicts a bighorn sheep impaled by arrows. Other Jornada Mogollon petroglyphs show various animals, lizards and a large number of snakes.

of drought. Before the end of the 1400s they had been replaced by the modern tribes of the region, who inherited many of their characteristics.

Whereas the northeastern coasts were primarily of interest to the English and French, it was the Spanish Empire that first made contact with the native tribes of the southwest. The Spanish were primarily interested in Mexico, undertaking fairly limited forays northwards at first. The same terrain that isolated the southwestern tribes from their neighbours contained Spanish expansion as well.

By the 1520s, Spanish settlers were raising horses in Mexico, and the horse was gradually spreading northwards as wild herds emerged. Enterprising tribes obtained these new animals by trade, raiding or catching a few animals from a wild herd, and began to make use of them. This ushered in a period of change in Native American society.

SOCIETY

In general, the tribes of the southwest were organized much like those elsewhere, with several extended families making up a band and multiple bands forming a tribe. Leadership was by popular acclaim, generally on an informal basis with chiefs emerging as they demonstrated their wisdom and charisma. Few tribes formally elected chiefs in this region.

Tribes that lived near reliable water sources built permanent settlements, sometimes digging canals to irrigate their crops. Those with a less predictable water source built stone barriers to trap or at least slow the floods that occurred when the rains came, and they planted their crops where they would benefit. Where water was scarce, a nomadic lifestyle dominated and food was gathered rather than farmed.

Pueblos

'Pueblo' was the name given by Spanish explorers to the settlements of the southwestern Native Americans. Built from stone or adobe, these took the form of large subdivided buildings capable of housing several families. The practice of building pueblos began around 750–900; before that the most common form of dwelling was a pit house constructed by digging a shallow pit and constructing a roof from whatever materials were available locally.

The construction of pueblos was common to many tribes of the southwest, which along with cultural similarities caused them to be collectively known as 'pueblo people'. Some pueblos were carved into rock faces, some constructed atop cliffs or on other defensive locations. Access to a ground-level pueblo was by means of a ladder that could be withdrawn into the building to deter intruders.

Above: Pueblo Bonito depicted around the time of its completion. It remains unclear whether it was a large settlement or a palace.

Construction of dwellings varied considerably. Some tribes used adobe (clay) bricks to build permanent houses; some built more modest structures with log supports and wattle-and-daub in between. Nomadic tribes or groups on the move made do with simple shelters such as lean-tos. The dry and generally warm climate made shelter less of a requirement than in colder northern latitudes.

NATIVE AMERICAN RELIGION

Native American groups developed a very different approach to religion than their counterparts in other regions. Indeed, some of the underlying concepts are sufficiently different that 'religion' may not be an appropriate word for the Native American belief system.

As with all hunter-gatherer societies, the tribes of North America were very close to the land and its creatures. As a result, spiritual belief and day-to-day life were closely intertwined. The supernatural world lay close to the mundane and was represented in it. Animals, birds and terrain such as mountains and rivers could all have spiritual significance. A rock that vaguely resembled a particular animal might be an important token if found during a vision quest.

There was no single 'Native American religion', and attempts by outsiders to create a simple explanation that fits all tribes' belief systems could not possibly succeed. Many tribes believed in a powerful creator or Great Spirit who made the world and everything that lives in it. Lesser spirits (manitou) could be contacted for assistance

or knowledge. The means by which this was achieved varied from tribe to tribe, although it usually involved consciousness-altering experiences such as fasting, great suffering or a ritual such as that of the sweat lodge.

There was no particular requirement about the size or construction of a sweat lodge so long as it could retain heat. A wikiup with thick hides covering it was as suitable as a pit house

or indeed any other structure. In some cultures the entrance faced east, as the rising sun was of spiritual significance. A totem such as a buffalo skull atop a pole marked the nearest anyone who was not a keeper of the sacred fire should approach, and around it would be placed sacred items.

The participants were usually required to prepare themselves before the ceremony, typically by fasting, and tobacco was an

important component. It might be smoked by participants or placed in the fire so that its smoke could act as a medium for contact with the spirit world. The ritual itself was a test of endurance, as four to seven stones were placed in the central pit and water poured over them to produce steam. Typically there would be four rounds to the ritual, with the stones reheated between them. Each round had a different significance.

A sweat lodge participant could leave at any time, and it was common to go outside between rounds to gain some relief from the heat. Some would remain inside the lodge for the entire duration. During the rounds, stories of creation and spiritual significance might be told, or the ceremony might be held in complete silence depending upon circumstances. The ritual was one of cleansing and renewal, and might be undertaken

Below: The Jemez Pueblo people have preserved their traditional language and ceremonies to the present day. Only some of their dances are shared with outsiders.

Above: Kachina dolls represented spirits and natural forces. They were used in ceremonies and also to teach tribe members about the spirit world.

Facing page: At the end of the Hopi snake dance, the snakes are released to carry prayers to the spirit world.

before or after a vision quest or whenever the participants felt the need to unburden their spirits or to ask for help and guidance from the spirit world.

Other ceremonies involved singing or dancing, such as the Sun Dance and the Ghost Dance ritual. What most had in common was active participation by everyone involved rather than mostly passive receipt as in the case of many formal religions. Actions in daily life also had religious significance, particularly acts of generosity. While ceremonies were important and generally required special effort, there was really no distinction between a Native American's daily life and his religion.

THE HOPI

Like many tribes of the southwest, the Hopi were descended from the Ancestral Pueblo people, inheriting

agricultural practices and the construction of their dwellings from the earlier pueblo builders. They were a generally peaceful people whose chiefs were spiritual leaders rather than warriors.

The Hopi made Kachina dolls to represent spirits, gods and natural phenomena, and they wore masks similar to those of the Kachina dolls during their ceremonies. Among their beliefs was the repeated destruction of the world by fire, ice and flood as a result of people losing their traditional ways and their reverence of the Great Spirit. The current, fourth, world was to be destroyed when certain signs were fulfilled, among them the coming of white men with their guns.

Contact with Spanish explorers came in 1540. The Hopi offered hospitality and there was no real conflict, although the efforts of Spanish missionaries to

spread Christianity were largely unsuccessful. Early Spanish colonization of the region did not at first trouble the Hopi, whose homes were in what is now northeastern Arizona and away

"…the Spanish Empire came to dominate the Hopi, making tribespeople work for them and attempting to force conversion to Catholicism."

from the river valleys favoured by the Spanish.

Over time, the Spanish Empire came to dominate the Hopi, making tribespeople work for them and attempting to force conversion to Catholicism. By 1680 the situation was bad enough that the peaceable Hopi joined the Zuni in a violent revolt against

Below: Hawikuh Pueblo was conquered in 1540 by the Spanish, who were hoping to find gold but had to be satisfied with a source of forced labour.

their oppressors. Their primary targets were religious institutions in what was in many ways similar to European crusades aimed at suppressing heresy. Priests and missionaries were killed, and the village of Awatovi was destroyed. Awatovi was the only Hopi settlement that had adopted Christianity on a large scale, allegedly in response to a miracle performed there. The men of the settlement were all killed and the women and children dispersed among other villages to be returned to their traditional ways. The lands of the Hopi were insufficiently valuable to the Spanish for much effort to be made at reconquest, so the tribe was able to return to its previous way of life disturbed only by raids from other Native Americans and the occasional Spanish expedition.

The Zuni were another Pueblo people with similar beliefs and way of life to the Hopi. Their oral

Shapes, Symbols and Medicine

The exact meaning of the term 'medicine' is hard to pin down. It is connected with supernatural power or what might be termed magic, and could be taken to refer to anything that had spiritual significance. Since every object, every creature and every person in the world had at least some significance, medicine was everywhere to a greater or lesser degree.

Those who understood the spirit world and the significance of objects in the mundane world could enhance their medicine or that of others, providing healing and protection, bringing rain or averting misfortune. Totems such as medicine bundles held great power and those entrusted with them were regarded as holy people. A medicine bundle contained several objects of spiritual significance and would not be opened without proper ritual.

Some shapes were of significance to the Native American tribes, notably the circle. Circles represented wholeness and rightness, and had strong medicine when used correctly. The round shape of a shield or the anchoring stones of a tipi were echoed in

the shape of the sun, which was considered a god by many tribes. Great circles of stones, sometimes referred to as medicine wheels, were created by many tribes. Their symbolism varied from one tribe to another, but all those that built them believed that they had great power.

Above: Some medicine bundles were personal, put together on the advice of a guardian spirit, while others were the property of a tribe and entrusted to a guardian.

histories included tales of how the Zuni had been underground and had emerged to take up residence in their current homes, much as the Hopi had taken refuge underground when the world was destroyed by fire.

The emergence of the United States onto the political scene benefited the Hopi, who requested

and received assistance against their enemies the Navajo. However, responses to US attempts to educate the tribe were mixed. Some chiefs welcomed the idea and went as far as to request a Western-style school for their people, while other groups felt the idea meant losing their traditional ways. Under-subscription of the school was 'solved' by forcing

pupils to attend, which caused great resentment. There was no large-scale conflict, however.

Overall, the Hopi lived up to their name, which translates roughly as 'peaceable ones'. So long as their way of life and their religion were not threatened, they were willing to live and let live. However, when required they could fight aggressively and take actions that might seem cruel to some, going so far as to kill their own people to remove a threat to their way of life.

THE MOJAVE

The Mojave people lived along the Colorado River valley, taking advantage of seasonal flooding to irrigate their crops. This diet was supplemented with hunting and fishing from the river. Their territory extended through what is now Arizona, California and Mexico, although man-made boundaries were meaningless; what mattered was that the river and its tributaries made farming possible.

The Mojave belonged to the River Yuman tribal group, and were allied to the Yuma although they were often hostile to other

Left: These chiefs of the Mojave people inherited their position from their fathers rather than being appointed in the manner of many other tribes.

"…man-made boundaries were meaningless; what mattered was that the river and its tributaries made farming possible."

tribes in the same area. Most tribes of the River Yuman and Upland Yuman groups were warlike, with the exception of the Havasupai, who were peaceable and – not coincidentally – lived in a well-watered canyon where agriculture could meet their needs.

Whereas many tribes were matrilineal, the Mojave traced their ancestry through the male line. Chiefdoms were hereditary, creating a more stratified society than many others. Although they lived in dispersed settlements they were highly organized in war, with a designated war chief and specialist warriors. In many tribes warriors fought as they pleased but the Mojave organized their men as archers or hand-to-hand fighters armed with war clubs.

Native American Shields

Many tribes used shields for protection in battle, but like most other aspects of the tribes' way of life they also had a spiritual purpose. A shield made from buffalo hide was entirely adequate to stop an opponent's blow with most weapons, and provided physical protection against arrows and even some early firearms. The medicine of a properly made shield greatly enhanced its protective quantities and could render the user immune to many forms of harm.

Shields were round and decorated with images chosen by the user. These were often animals, birds or insects, and might be connected to the warrior's spirit guide if he had one. Additional items such as eagle feathers or buffalo hair made the shield look more impressive and enhanced its medicine. Some shields were extremely powerful items that took on an importance beyond just their user, in a similar manner to holy relics or magical objects of Western mythology. Miniature shields were sometimes carried by warriors for supernatural protection.

Right: The round shape of this Comanche shield was important for its spiritual protection. Circles were considered sacred by many tribes.

By the 1850s, white settlers had begun to encroach upon the lands of the Mojave, which could support only a fairly small population. Conflict was inevitable as the Mojave tried to expel the settlers, and at the end of the decade the United States government decided to establish a fort – to be known as Fort Mojave – in Mojave territory. Realizing they could not oppose the force sent to establish the fort, the Mohave withdrew and were soon afterward offered a bleak choice between accepting US authority or face a war they could not win.

Fort Mojave eventually became a school for Native American

children, which they were forced to attend. As with other such schools the use of their native language or following traditional customs were strictly forbidden and harshly punished. The choice made by the Mojave was between the slow extinction of their culture or the rapid destruction of their tribe; there were no good answers.

THE NAVAJO

The Navajo migrated into the southwest region from the Pacific Northwest, probably around 1400. They retained their Athabaskan-family language even though they adopted the lifestyle of the southwestern tribes. They did not build adobe pueblos however, but instead used pit houses called hogans. A hogan was built by digging a flat-floored

"Hogans had spiritual significance as well as being homes, and had to be dedicated once built. If a person died in a hogan it would be destroyed..."

pit then creating a roof out of timbers covered with turf, mud or sometimes stone. The entryway to a hogan faced east so that the occupants could greet the rising sun. Hogans had spiritual significance as well as being homes, and had to be dedicated once built. If a person died in a hogan it would be destroyed, as no one would live in such a structure.

The Navajo occupied territory in what is now Arizona, Colorado,

Below: The move from hunting game to herding sheep was a natural one for the Navajo, though it did not take place quickly or completely.

New Mexico and Utah. They were semi-nomadic farmers who supplemented their agricultural production with hunting, and later began farming sheep and goats. They took part in the Pueblo Revolt of 1680, attacking Spanish holdings with some success. For the most part, however, they were as willing to trade with the Spanish as with their Native American neighbours. Navajo warriors sometimes skirmished with Spanish settlers, but just as often banded together with them to resist attacks by the Apache or Comanche.

When the United States gained control over the region, the Navajo

Code Talkers

During the World Wars, Native American languages were used as a near-unbreakable code by the US military. The most well known of these 'code talkers' were Navajo, whose language was incomprehensible to an enemy who managed to listen in on US communications. The languages of other tribes and cultural groups were used in both World Wars for similar purposes, both as a formal policy and on an ad-hoc basis.

Above: Although any code can be broken eventually, enemies who intercepted transmissions made by the Navajo 'code talkers' would have to decipher an entire – and very complex – language, before progressing to decyphering the code.

made a treaty that permitted the creation of military posts, although the peace was uneasy. Relations deteriorated and conflict became increasingly common, culminating in an expedition by militia from New Mexico in 1860. The destruction of villages and crops, in combination with serious casualties, weakened the Navajo considerably, as did another expedition in 1863.

In 1864, in part due to requests for assistance from the Hopi, the US military rounded up the Navajo and forced them to relocate to the area around Fort Sumner in New Mexico. This march became known as The Long Walk and inflicted further losses on people who were unprepared for its hardships. Navajo settlements were destroyed as part of the campaign to remove them from their homeland.

Internment at Fort Sumner was hard for the Navajo, partly because the area was unable to support their population and partly because some members of the Apache tribe were interned with them; the two had a long history of conflict. The Navajo eventually returned to their homelands, but were greatly diminished by their hardships.

THE SHOSHONE AND THE COMANCHE

The Shoshone occupied territory from California to Wyoming, and were divided into four main groups. Their population was highly dispersed most of the time, typically with extended families living a nomadic existence wherever food could be gathered or hunted. From around 1680, the Northern and Wind River Shoshone tribes adopted the horse and began hunting buffalo on the plains.

The Comanche were an offshoot of the Wind River Shoshone, whose warlike ways enabled them to move into Texas and enrich themselves by raiding. They were especially fierce, and deliberately enhanced their fearsome reputation by torturing captives. The weapons of the Comanche were traditional – bows, lances and war clubs, and rifles once they could obtain them. Shields were used for protection and were often buried with their owners.

The Comanche were early horse-masters, capturing wild mustangs and training them as well as breeding them for their own use and for trade to other clans.

Below: The Comanche made themselves 'lords of the plains' by their early adoption of the horse and exploitation of the advantages it offered.

Indeed, the Comanche were among the foremost horse-traders of the plains and introduced several other tribes to the benefits of riding. Horses were a status symbol and would be painted after a battle to

"...the Comanche were among the foremost horse-traders of the plains and introduced several other tribes to the benefits of riding."

Below: The only counter to Comanche raids was to create a similarly mobile and hard-hitting force. The Texas Rangers were officially formed in 1835, but had existed for some time previously.

show the owner's achievements. Upon his death his horses would all be killed and his favourite buried with him.

The Comanche were allied to the Ute at the time they split from the Shoshone, and were enemies of

the Apache from around 1700. The Comanche–Ute alliance dissolved into conflict in the 1730s, leading to a half-century of conflict. Their numbers declined as a result of smallpox epidemics in the early 1800s, but by the 1830s they were still powerful enough to survive conflict with the Cheyenne and Arapaho, and with US troops at more or less the same time.

The Texas Rangers were formed to fight the Comanche, which in turn influenced the development of some of the world's most famous firearms. A captain of the rangers approached Samuel Colt about creating a powerful revolver for use on horseback, leading to the introduction of the Colt Walker revolver. Among the rangers' stipulations was that the weapon had to fire a round powerful enough to stop a horse.

The 'Peace Pipe'

The smoking of tobacco – sometimes mixed with other substances – was an important part of Native American ceremony, although the details varied considerably from one tribe to another. In many cases, the smoke was considered to carry prayers, questions or requests to the spirit world. Ceremonial pipes were used

for the purpose, causing Europeans to mistakenly call them 'peace pipes', since the only time they saw them used was a parlay or the agreement of a treaty. In fact the pipe might be smoked on many other occasions. Pipe designs varied depending on tribe or purpose, with some very ornate examples existing. Some pipes were built into

Above: Like many aspects of Native American culture, the ceremonial smoking of tobacco was only partially understood by outsiders, leading to misconceptions like the 'peace pipe'.

a ceremonial tomahawk while others were adorned with significant items such as feathers, hair or skin from powerful animals.

Right: The Comanche were able to prevent settlers moving through their lands for several generations, and even depleted by disease they represented a formidable force.

"Depleted by disease, the Comanche could not repeat this exploit, although they took part in raids against the Santa Fe Trail with their allies, and the full-scale war that followed."

Conflict between the Comanche and the Texas Rangers intensified when several Comanche leaders were killed in what became known as the Council House Fight. This was a peace parlay held in March 1840, which went badly awry. In response, Chief Buffalo Hump launched a large-scale raid – the Great Raid of 1840 – that caused immense destruction. The Comanche were able to overrun the town of Victoria, although the defenders held out in fortified buildings.

The Great Raid netted the Comanche around 2000 horses and mules, and by August 1840 Buffalo Hump's force was outside Linville, a port serving San Antonio. The town was looted and burned, with the spoils loaded aboard the captured mules. Finally satisfied that the Council House Fight had been avenged, Buffalo Hump led his warriors homeward.

A force of Texas Rangers and militia set up an ambush at Plum Creek, but delayed springing it to wait for reinforcements. Nevertheless, they were able to catch the rearmost elements of the Comanche force by surprise. A running fight developed, in which

the Texans claimed the Comanche suffered heavy casualties. The exact figure is debatable, and the Comanche did escape with most of their plunder, but the Texans claimed victory since their enemies retreated before them.

Depleted by disease, the Comanche could not repeat this exploit, although they took part in raids against the Santa Fe Trail with their allies, and the full-scale war that followed. In 1865 the Comanche signed a treaty with the US government granting them territory in Oklahoma in return for their ancestral lands, bringing

to an end a short war against the USA. The treaty quickly collapsed and fighting continued until 1867. A new treaty was also unsuccessful, and the Comanche became involved in the Red River War alongside the Arapaho, Cheyenne and Kiowa.

THE APACHE

The ancestors of the Apache migrated south from what is now Canada to adopt a nomadic lifestyle around the Rio Grande. Elements of the tribe moved into Kansas around 1700 and tried their hand at farming, but were driven

off by the Comanche. They spread out into Texas, New Mexico and Arizona, and began competing with Spanish settlers for land. This conflict escalated until the 1740s, when an agreement was reached. As a symbol of the new peace, an Apache chief buried a hatchet – the origins of that figure of speech.

In time, relations soured and conflict began once again. The tribe was nomadic and unconcerned with the territorial boundaries imagined by others, thus was active in Mexico and the United States. In the 1830s the Mexican authorities put a bounty on Apache scalps,

COPYRIGHT
1886, By C. S. Fly,
Tombstone, Ariz.

"…his enemies often called upon their patron saint – Saint Jerome – to save them, which resulted in Goyathlay gaining a nickname by which he is better known to history: Geronimo."

Above: Geronimo (at right, with a long rifle) gained his nickname from the frightened cries of his enemies; perhaps the ultimate accolade for a warrior.

and the ensuing conflict saw the emergence of a warrior named Goyathlay who was also a medicine man. Such was the reputation of Goyathlay that his enemies often called upon their patron saint – Saint Jerome – to save them, which resulted in Goyathlay gaining a nickname by which he is better known to history: Geronimo.

The Jicarilla Apache and their allies, the Ute, opposed the opening of the Santa Fe Trail from Missouri to New Mexico, resulting in the Jicarilla War of 1849–54. The conflict began with attacks on wagons and escalated until in 1853 a force of US dragoons engaged and was defeated by a superior force of Apache and Ute warriors. Accounts of the battle vary; some claim the dragoons were ambushed while others suggest the US force was tempted into a rash attack. Both were common Native American tactics. A larger action took place in Ojo Caliente Canyon in April 1854, in which US forces were victorious. After this the war wound down and finally petered out after some final skirmishes.

Another great warrior emerged among the Apache in the 1860s, when the discovery of gold caused conflict to break out between the Chiricahua Apache and white settlers and miners. The chief of the Chiricahua, Cochise, was accused of inciting or perhaps leading raids that had in fact been carried out by another Apache band. He managed to escape an attempt to capture him by fighting his way out of a US Army camp armed with a knife.

Led by Cochise and his father-in-law Mangas Coloradas, the Apache made war on the

Above: Cochise led the Apache in their war against the United States government until 1872, when he agreed a treaty restricting his people to a reservation.

Below right: Apache warriors armed with rifle, spear and bow, photographed in 1873. For all their advantages, firearms never completely supplanted the traditional weapons.

white settlements in the region. Distracted by the tensions that would ultimately lead to the Civil War, the US government made a patchy and half-hearted response that could not match the mobility and aggression of the Apache.

The Apache fought against both sides in the American Civil War. At the Battle of Dragoon Springs in May 1862 they attacked Confederate troops escorting Union prisoners and made off with horses and livestock. A few days later Confederate troops recaptured most of the animals after inflicting a defeat on the Apache. An agreement was then made to become co-belligerent against the Union.

In July the advance guard of a union column moving east from California was attacked as it marched through Apache Pass. Mangas Coloradas and Cochise – and possibly Geronimo – led around 500 Apache warriors who

had constructed a fortified position across the line of march. The Union force was short of water and needed to reach Dragoon Springs to resupply.

Retreat was not viable, as it would require a long march back to the nearest water source, so the Union force made an initial attempt to break through that was repulsed. Once deployed, the supporting Union artillery was ineffective at first but was able to gradually advance despite rifle fire. Faced with increasingly effective shooting the Apache withdrew after nightfall, returning the next day to resume the fight. They fell back in the face of further bombardment, permitting the Union force to take possession of the springs.

The Apache had no experience of facing artillery up to this point, and were demoralized by it. This may have been a factor in their decision to accept an invitation

to parlay. Mangas Coloradas was taken hostage despite the supposed safe conduct of a parlay, and was killed allegedly while trying to escape. The decision was then taken that the Apache and the Navajo must be moved to a reservation. The latter were forced to go to Fort Sumner in what became known as their Long Walk. Conflict with the Apache continued on a smaller scale, until Cochise agreed to accept a reservation in the Dragoon Hills in 1872.

BATTLES AT ADOBE WALLS

The first and second battles of Adobe Walls were named for the ruins of a trading post in northern Texas. The conflict stemmed from attacks on wagon trains crossing the Great Plains, which had escalated as the Civil War drew troops from the region. In November 1864 a punitive expedition under 'Kit' Carson was sent against the Kiowa and Comanche, with Apache and Ute scouts assisting.

The pattern was a familiar one – the column was to locate villages of the target tribes and destroy them to force the tribes into submission. This apparently went well enough at first, with a Kiowa village surprised and its people forced to scatter. However, large numbers of Comanche were also in the area and converged on the column, forcing Carson to make for the refuge of Adobe Walls. There, his force made a stand against perhaps three or four times its number.

It seemed that the fire of artillery might again prove decisive, but although dismayed at

the first shots the warriors renewed their attack and were joined by ever-increasing numbers of their allies. The Kiowa and Comanche proved hard to hit as they clung to the necks of their ponies, at times firing from beneath the horse's chest as they galloped by. One of their tribes had learned army bugle calls and obtained a bugle, using it to make false calls in the hope of spreading confusion.

Eventually Carson's force was able to make a fighting withdrawal and rejoin its supply train. The US

Above: Mangas Coloradas was treacherously taken prisoner and then murdered by his captors. Such actions served mainly to prolong the conflict by reducing trust in any parlay attempt.

War Paint

The colours and symbols used in war paint had many meanings, which varied from one tribe to another. In general, designs could serve one of three purposes. They might grant an ability, such as magical speed or agility; they could symbolize previous achievements or current intentions – such as a willingness to fight to the death – or they might be used as what amounts to rank insignia.

The leader of a war party could be recognized by painted markings on his face, while a warrior might display his previous battle achievements in the hope of intimidating his enemies. Paint could be self-applied, but was often used as part of preparation ceremonies before a raid or battle, in which case a medicine man might apply it as part of the ritual.

Paint served other purposes, some of them ritualistic and some mundane. Paint might be applied in preparation for a ceremony or ritual, but could also be used on a daily basis to act as a form of insect repellent. It was made from a variety of substances including clay, berries, shells or flowers, and was stored as a dried powder.

Left: Along with the headdress and decoration on other items, war paint served to demonstrate status, allowing members of a war party to quickly locate and identify their leaders.

claimed the battle as a victory since the target village was destroyed, but the strategic outcome was that the Comanche and Kiowa remained in control of the area. By 1874 that situation had changed little, but attempts were being made to restore the remains of Adobe Walls as a base for the mass buffalo hunting then taking place. An alliance of Comanche, Kiowa and Cheyenne warriors arrived at the post in June 1874 with the intent of destroying it. Their initial attack was repulsed after close-quarters gunfire in which repeating carbines and revolvers proved invaluable, after which a situation akin to a siege ensued.

Long-range fire was exchanged but no further massed assaults took place, and after a spectacularly lucky rifle shot killed a warrior who was thought to be well out of range, the attackers fell back further. As additional hunters arrived and slipped into the post the odds of success diminished and the siege petered out after some minor skirmishing.

THE RED RIVER WAR

The second battle of Adobe Walls, along with other skirmishes in the region, prompted the US government to launch a major expedition against the tribes of the plains. The US Army threw massive resources at the campaign, marching columns across the plains in search of settlements to destroy. The tribes were often able to avoid contact, but were forced to keep moving their villages with the result that great hardships were suffered even when combat did not occur.

Above: Quanah Parker is widely referred to as the last chief of the Comanche. After success as a war leader, he became an emissary for his people as they began a new life on the reservation.

Some villages were caught, but even then most of the population were able to escape while the warriors skirmished with the US troops. However, food and possessions were lost each time, weakening the tribes until one by one they were forced to surrender. The last major force of Native Americans on the southern Great Plains was a Comanche band under Quanah Parker, who surrendered in June 1875.

GERONIMO'S WAR

Cochise died in 1874, and the treaty he agreed in 1872 was abrogated by the US government. The Apache were ordered to move to a new reservation. The San Carlos reservation was located on poor land where life was hard for

Right: Geronimo (centre left) was not inclined to trust General Crook's attempt at a parlay, but by 1886 he was leading a handful of die-hard supporters and had no alternative but to surrender.

Below: Despite tremendous odds, Victorio's band conducted an initially successful guerrilla war using horses captured from their enemies to provide superior mobility.

the tribes, and internal conflict was inevitable as different bands of Apache – like many tribes – were often at odds with one another.

Finding the situation intolerable, a leader named Victorio gathered around 200 supporters and began a move to Ojo Caliente in New Mexico. He had been promised his people could settle there before he surrendered, although the promise was not kept. A successful skirmish with US cavalry gained Victorio's band a number of horses and pack animals, and encouraged others to leave the reservation.

Attacks on settlers in the area prompted a massive US military response, along with the formation of militias. One such group was defeated by Victorio's band, which drew a response from the US cavalry. Lured into an ambush in Las Animas Canyon, the cavalry became engaged in a protracted firefight with Victorio's warriors. The arrival of reinforcements did not improve the situation; the initial attack was repulsed and this force, too, became bogged down in a firefight. Eventually the cavalry withdrew.

Victorio was killed by Mexican troops in 1880, and leadership of his force fell to Geronimo's brother-in-law Nana. Despite his advanced age – Nana is known to have been around 80 or perhaps older at the beginning of the campaign – he attracted followers from several tribes and led an extremely successful campaign of raiding over a wide area.

Nana's followers evaded the large forces sent against them and resupplied themselves with horses from the posts and settlements they raided. Nana surrendered

in 1886, living another 10 years afterwards. While Nana was raising hell on the plains, other Apache were launching their own raids. Geronimo led a guerrilla campaign until captured in 1877, at which time he was taken to the San Carlos reservation. Four years later, suspicious that he was to be arrested by US troops, Geronimo led around 700 Apache off the reservation. He was found in Mexico with his followers and persuaded to return.

An attempt was made to improve conditions on the

Above: Edd Ladd of the Apache people and Indian Commissioner Cato Sells pictured in 1920. By this time conflict within the United States was more or less over.

reservation but attracted censure from an 'Indian-hating' press and ultimately was derailed. Geronimo left the reservation again, and thousands of troops backed up by an even greater number of militia were mobilized to locate him. When finally caught after more skirmishes and raids, Geronimo was leading just two dozen warriors. He was made a prisoner of war, finally dying in 1909.

LAST BATTLES ON THE PLAINS

The last large-scale battle between tribes occurred at Massacre Canyon in August 1873 between the Pawnee and the Sioux. The two had a long history of conflict – indeed, one of the Sioux chiefs was named Pawnee Killer. The Pawnee were conducting a buffalo hunt in territory the Sioux considered theirs, and having recently been persuaded not to raid the Ute

in retaliation for an attack the warriors of the tribe were spoiling for a fight.

A party of hunters moving ahead of the main Pawnee group were ambushed, after which the Sioux began firing down from the canyon walls. The Pawnee began to retreat, their warriors fighting back as best they could, but the whole Pawnee hunting party – including women and children – was outnumbered by Sioux warriors.

The US authorities used the incident to strengthen their claim that the Native Americans must remain on their reservations for their own safety and deployed troops whose presence did nothing to deter further raiding. The Pawnee and the Sioux eventually made peace in 1925.

The last conflict involving US troops was a series of skirmishes with Apache warriors lasting until the 1920s. Conflict between the Apache and Mexican troops did not end until 1933. These were mostly small-scale raids by groups living in Mexico; the surrender of Geronimo in 1886 marked the end of large-scale conflict in the area.

The last real conflict to take place is known as Posey's War, in which Chief Posey led his followers off the reservation and took refuge in the mountains of Utah. His people, the Ute, had skirmished occasionally with US forces as they tried to retain their ancestral lands. This time they were opposed by a local militia, and gunfire was exchanged as the tribespeople tried to break contact. The uprising dissipated, and with it the last armed opposition to the loss of traditional lands or ways of life.

Hunting Buffalo with Spears

Before the introduction of the horse, buffalo hunting was a difficult business. Even the most powerful bow could fail to produce a quick kill, and a wounded buffalo might wander for a great distance before finally succumbing to its injuries. The spear offered a more certain kill and this remained in use after bows became available.

The typical Native American spear had a wooden haft and a head of sharpened bone or stone, later replaced with metal in some but by no means all cases. Spears could be thrown with or without a throwing-stick to increase velocity but were also used as hand weapons.

The problem of getting close enough to use a spear on a buffalo was solved by confining the animals in a buffalo pound. This was an enclosure set up as a killing ground, into which buffalo were chased by warriors – although Chief Poundmaker was said to be able to entice the buffalo into the pound using magic.

However they got there, the trapped animals were then speared at close range by waiting warriors. An alternative to this method was to frighten the buffalo so that they stampeded over a cliff or into difficult terrain. Stuck or injured animals could then be finished off with spears.

This necessitated getting very close to an injured and frightened animal with the mass to cause severe injuries even if it did not deliberately attack the hunter, so it required skill and daring. The same adept handling of the spear while maintaining situational awareness was a useful skill in battle.

Below: The introduction of the horse enabled hunters to chase down their quarry, making a kill with a spear more likely. The buffalo hunt still required a high level of skill.

Tribes of the West

The people who would become Native Americans migrated onto the continent by way of what is now Alaska, western Canada and the Pacific Northwest. The mountain ranges of the region channelled initial expansion and would later come to determine the territory of tribes. The coastal plains, high plateaux and deep valleys offered plentiful game and raw materials in the form of timber from the region's extensive forests.

This permitted a lifestyle not dissimilar to that of the northeastern woodlands, although the diverse terrain of the western continent influenced the local tribes in many ways. Further south the dryer and warmer climate of what is now California caused tribes to adopt a different way of life to their northern cousins.

The west is tectonically active, and echoes of its volcanoes and earthquakes can be seen in the local tribes' myths and creation stories. Many have tales of destruction by fire or flooding, which could well have come about as a result of the glaciers melting as they first migrated through this region. The Ice Age certainly left its mark on the west of the continent, leaving behind coastal fjords and deep valleys containing glacial deposits.

WAVES OF MIGRATION

There are several theories about how the early tribes migrated into the Americas. It is likely that migration took place in waves, with smaller groups wandering across the Beringia land bridge in between these mass migrations. The last wave of migrants remained in the far north, largely because the more hospitable land to the south was already occupied. These tribes continued to use the same means of surviving and feeding themselves that they had during the migration or while they were dwelling in the vastness of Siberia.

Left: Chief Joseph was a great champion of his people both in war and in peace. He is said to have died of a broken heart, unable ever to return home.

Above: Many of the northern tribes used temporary shelters in the summer and more substantial dwellings during the coldest months.

Other groups pushed south and east, eventually becoming the ancestors of the modern tribes. Their way of life adapted to their new conditions, creating cultural changes and requiring new ways of thinking in order to overcome

> *"...People moved between communities – not always voluntarily – along with ideas and designs for tools and weapons."*

problems encountered on the move or in a new home. However, no tribe existed completely in isolation. People moved between communities – not always voluntarily – along with ideas and designs for tools and weapons.

Some of what was learned by the tribes moving east and south was passed back to those who remained in the far north or who followed on behind.

Nor did migration ever completely stop. Tribes that found a suitable place might settle down for many decades, but conflict or changing climate conditions could force a new movement. This would in turn disrupt other tribes encountered on the march, perhaps causing further migrations. Early on the general trend was east and south, but after the arrival of Europeans on the eastern shores of the Americas many tribes were pushed westwards.

THE ALASKAN AND ATHABASKAN PEOPLE

The indigenous people of Alaska were largely descended from the last arrivals across the Beringia land bridge. Many were Inuit, Yupik or Aleuts, related to the tribes of the far north who migrated to the east. Those that dwelled on the coast excelled at fishing from canoes and at hunting seals, while those living inland hunted or herded reindeer for meat and hides. Their primary hunting tools – and thus their main weapons if forced to fight – were harpoons used for fishing and bows for hunting on land.

These groups were distinct but related, and at times have been referred to collectively as 'Eskimo'. This term is thought by some to be derogatory, although its mistaken connotations of 'eaters of raw flesh' have been debunked. They were

The Potlatch Ceremony

Above: The Potlatch ceremony was such an important part of Native American culture that it was outlawed by the US government in the hope of forcing assimilation.

A potlatch was a festival that might be held for many reasons. Even a fairly modest potlatch was a major affair, with every guest given an identical gift and great care taken over preparation of food. The potlatch would include dancing and tales of a traditional nature as well as less formal storytelling. The potlatch ceremony was outlawed from 1885 to 1951, although many tribes continued to hold their ceremonies in defiance of the law.

A potlatch was an opportunity to demonstrate generosity, and it might be held for no other reason than this. However, ceremonies were often held to mark some important occasion such as weddings or births or even to restore the dignity of an important person who had suffered some misfortune or loss of face. Such was the expense involved with a large potlatch that tribes sometimes manoeuvred their enemies into holding one in order to deplete their resources or demonstrate their weakness and inability to do it properly.

also related to similar people still dwelling in Siberia.

The Athabaskan peoples were distinct from the Inuit and their close relatives but related to one another by a common language family, much as Algonquian was spoken in various forms in the east of the continent. The name comes from Lake Athabasca in the northwest of Saskatchewan, Canada, and represents a territorial association of the people who spoke these languages rather than a tribal affiliation. The Northern Athabaskan people were native to

Left: Taken around 1868, this photograph demonstrates the melding of cultures and habits of dress taking place in Tlingit society.

> "*The Athabaskan peoples were distinct from the Inuit and their close relatives but related to one another by a common language family.*"

what is now Alaska and the Yukon, with a matrilineal society. Speakers of the Pacific Coast Athabaskan languages and the Southern Athabaskan languages were located down the Pacific coast as far south as what is now California.

THE TLINGIT AND HAIDA

The Tlingit and the related Haida were native to the coast and islands of Alaska and Canada. The Tlingit spoke an Athabaskan-related language and had a matrilineal society, with clans tracing their ancestry back to a legendary founder. The organization of the Tlingit was very loose, with villages being essentially self-governing and tribal leaders very rare.

These tribes were warlike, with the possession of slaves taken in battle serving as an indicator of status. They were equally adept at fighting on land or at sea, using large canoes for both hunting sea mammals and fighting other tribes. In these canoes they ranged up and down the Pacific coast, raiding settlements as far south as what is now California.

The Tlingit used their traditional weapons – bows, spears and various forms of club – until firearms became available. They also made extensive use of body armour fashioned from thick hide or wooden slats. Once they began encountering firearms the Tlingit took to enhancing their armour with coins – typically of Chinese origin – in the hope of creating at least a measure of protection from bullets. Tlingit war helmets were carved from spruce, with elaborate designs reflecting the history of their clan and the deeds of its founder. These helmets had a ceremonial as well as practical function, and offered good protection from hand weapons and even musketballs.

RUSSIAN INCURSIONS

The earliest known reference to Alaska in Russian documents is dated to 1648, noting the accidental discovery of land by an expedition headed elsewhere. It was almost a century later that Russian explorers set out to discover the lands to their east, landing on Alaskan islands. These expeditions brought back samples of sea otter pelts that sparked an interest in creating a fur trade across the Bering Strait, and soon

trappers and traders began to set up operations.

The Russian fur traders preferred to obtain their pelts from local hunters, particularly the Aleut of the Aleutian Islands. As the fur trade grew, the employment of Aleut turned to exploitation and even slavery, with groups forced to relocate wherever the fur traders wanted them to work and to undertake hazardous trips out to sea in bad weather. Revolts against this oppression were harshly put down, and in addition disease epidemics killed off most of the Aleut.

In the 1780s, deliberate colonization of Alaska by Russian settlers began despite resistance from local tribes that had no answer to the warships Russia could deploy against their canoes and coastal villages. Colonies were founded, but supporting them was difficult and the fur trade began to peter out as a result of excessive hunting. Eventually the Russian possessions in Alaska were abandoned or sold to the USA.

Chief among those that resisted the Russian incursion were the Tlingit, who may have attacked

Below and above: The carved wooden helmets of the Tlingit had ceremonial and spiritual significance, but they could also stop a bullet or a blow from a war club.

Facing page: The Tlingit people came into conflict with Russian fur traders, who wisely decided that friendly relations were more profitable than war.

Russian explorers in 1741. They certainly fought against a Russian expedition of 1793. During this clash the Russians found their muskets were unable to penetrate the wooden helmets of the Tlingit, although they were still able to drive the attackers off.

Peaceful relations were established for a time, but mistreatment of the local population caused the Tlingit to revolt against them and destroy the fort at Baranov Island. The Tlingit had access to firearms by this time but could not deal with cannon mounted on Russian ships. Despite this, they destroyed other forts and the Russians decided to make peace with the tribe. A series of feasts and the giving of gifts secured friendly relations that were largely maintained until the Russian government sold its interests in Alaska to the USA in 1867 and withdrew.

THE CHINOOK

The Chinook were native to what is now Oregon and Washington states, ranging far and wide on trading expeditions. The tribes of the northwest traded extensively with one another, developing a trade language known as Chinook Jargon. This language evolved over time, picking up words from various Native American languages and later English and French. Their traders maintained contact with

Tobacco and Smudging Rituals

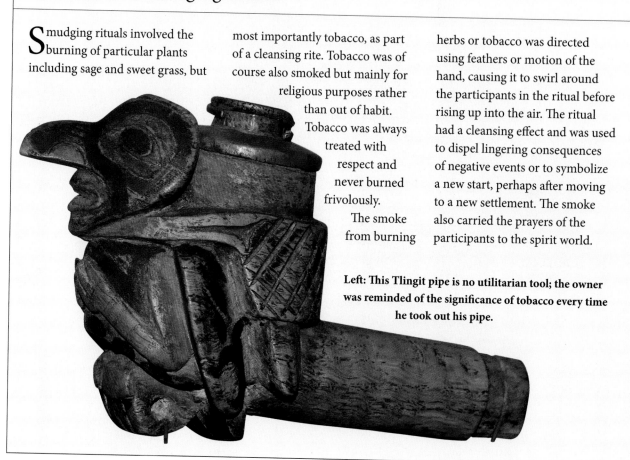

Smudging rituals involved the burning of particular plants including sage and sweet grass, but most importantly tobacco, as part of a cleansing rite. Tobacco was of course also smoked but mainly for religious purposes rather than out of habit. Tobacco was always treated with respect and never burned frivolously.

The smoke from burning herbs or tobacco was directed using feathers or motion of the hand, causing it to swirl around the participants in the ritual before rising up into the air. The ritual had a cleansing effect and was used to dispel lingering consequences of negative events or to symbolize a new start, perhaps after moving to a new settlement. The smoke also carried the prayers of the participants to the spirit world.

Left: This Tlingit pipe is no utilitarian tool; the owner was reminded of the significance of tobacco every time he took out his pipe.

the tribes of the Great Plains and those in the southwest, facilitating the movement of items and ideas between these distant people and those of the northwest.

The rivers of their territory were highly important to the Chinook, who made extensive use of the Columbia and its tributaries in their trade expeditions. Salmon from the rivers was an important part of their diet, and the first salmon run of the year was an important ceremonial occasion.

Like many other tribes, the Chinook used the traditional weapons of bow and spear, with warriors sometimes making use

Below: Spear-fishing requires excellent timing and great precision. This Chinook fisherman will have honed his skills for many years before he could reliably feed himself by this method.

of a thick hide breastplate. This was reinforced with wood and bark, giving protection against arrows. Bows were used mainly for harassing fire, with most combat being carried out hand-to-hand or at very close range with spears and harpoons. The Chinook were skilled at spear-fishing and could turn their skills against human targets if necessary. They were also wealthy enough that at times they paid or otherwise induced warriors from other tribes to fight for them.

The war club was also used by many warriors. Various designs were employed, typically with a stone striking head on both sides of the shaft. These versatile weapons were capable of putting any opponent out of action, but in a raid or the closing stages of a battle they could be used to deliver less lethal strikes in the hope of obtaining slaves to be kept or traded.

THE YUMA

The territory of the Yuma lay on the Colorado River in what is now Arizona and California. The Yuma were skilled in warfare but were also traders who maintained links with tribes on the Pacific coast and far inland. They practised seasonal agriculture, taking advantage of floods to irrigate their land, but they primarily supported themselves by fishing from rafts, supplemented with some hunting and gathering of wild plants.

The Yuma built light structures known as kiich, consisting of a frame made from wooden poles covered in plant fibre. These were often dug into the ground to create a variant on the pit house design. The main problem facing the Yuma

Above: A musician of the Yuma people, who were initially friendly to Spanish settlers. They later fought against Spanish then US attempts to control their lands.

Totem Pole

The totem pole is primarily associated with tribes of the northwest. It was carved in likenesses of real and mythical creatures, people and elements of the natural world such as the sun and moon. The totems near the bottom of the pole were the most significant, with those at the top often identifying the tribe that carved the pole.

Totem poles could fulfil many roles. They served as a record of the tribe's history or memorialized a particular event, and were used to mark graves or celebrate the deeds of a particularly notable individual. A totem pole might also be created to bring shame on an individual or tribe, ensuring their misdeeds were known to anyone who knew how to interpret the totems.

They could also signify ownership and might be placed in front of a chief's house or carved into it. A pole might mark the boundaries of a tribe's territory or signify a claim to ownership of land, particularly a stretch of water.

Making a pole was a long and involved process requiring skilled craftsmanship and an understanding of how totems were created. There were rules for how the eyes of certain creatures were to be carved, and how mythical and normal creatures might be combined to create certain meanings. The ability to create such a pole depended on prosperity – a tribe that was expending all its efforts on subsistence would not have time to produce such a complex item – and thus the totem pole was also a status symbol.

Above: Totem poles claiming ownership over a stretch of land or water could reduce the chances of conflict by warning off hunters who might stray into unfriendly territory.

was excess heat rather than cold, and this semi-subterranean construction was cooler than a surface dwelling. Likewise, the Yuma needed few clothes; men typically wore little more than a breechcloth.

The Yuma were contacted by the Spanish as they moved into the area in 1540, but had little interaction for the next two centuries. In the 1770s Spanish colonists moved into their territory. Initially relations were not hostile – a Yuman chief and some of his people were baptized and missions were set up. However, the Spanish Empire treated the Yuma as dominated people and was not a kind master.

YUMA REBELLION

The Yuma rebelled in 1781, the flashpoint being the destruction of their crops by livestock allowed to wander freely by a Spanish expedition. Enraged that the Spanish did not care about the loss of their food, the Yuma and their allies attacked the missions and destroyed them. Although attempts were made to regain control over the area, the Yuma successfully resisted Spanish domination.

After the region passed to the control of the United States settlement of the area continued, along with a rush to California in the hope of finding gold, and tensions inevitably rose. These were not restricted to a simple white man/Native American conflict as the Yuma were living in a place and time where tensions ran high between some states and the Federal government, as well as between different groups of white settlers.

The situation was aggravated by the massacre in 1850 of both tribespeople and settlers using a river ferry that the Yuma had set up. The ferry allowed the Yuma to profit from the flow of settlers and gold-hunters headed to and from California, and was attacked in an indiscriminate act of banditry rather than motivated by hate or conflict over territory.

The raiders attacked other Yuma settlements for profit and were eliminated by Yuma warriors as a result. The incident developed into conflict with the state of

> "Enraged that the Spanish did not care about the loss of their food, the Yuma and their allies attacked the missions and destroyed them."

California, which raised a militia and set them against the Yuma. The Yuma wore down the expedition with guerrilla tactics, forcing the survivors to return home.

Late in 1850 the Yuma agreed a treaty that permitted troops to be stationed to protect the river crossing and to deter further banditry. Despite difficulties in keeping the post supplied, its garrison were able to help the Yuma when their crops failed. Despite generally good relations with the troops at the post, in 1851 the Yuma took up arms against the USA. They had been assured that disaffected whites in Mexico and California would join them. Instead they opposed the revolt,

Facing page: This photograph of Chief Miguel of the Yuma was taken around 1885–90. By this time, the 'Indian Wars' were over and the tribes' traditional way of life severely restricted.

Above: Like many tribes, the Yuma were presented with tools and supplies intended to turn them into farmers tied to a particular stretch of land.

which was led by a warrior of the Cupeno people named Antonio Garra.

Garra was captured and subsequently executed, and an expedition set out in early 1852 for the Yuma fort. The garrison there had been greatly reduced

"...the Nez Percé shared close linguistic connections with the Cayuse and the Molala."

due to supply problems, and the Yuma had taken advantage of the situation to wreck the fort and its surroundings. A series of skirmishes took place in which the

Yuma harassed supply convoys but avoided combat with columns sent to engage them. Villages vacated as a column approached were destroyed, but the settlements of the Yuma were temporary anyway so the action had little effect.

The tactics used by the Yuma and their allies paid off at the Battle of the Gila River. Facing a column of infantry, the Yuma harassed the much larger force with rifle fire and arrows until its commander decided to charge, at which point the warriors dispersed and vanished into the surrounding terrain. Other expeditions met the same response or were simply evaded by the more mobile Yuma.

The Yuma War came to an end in 1853, although the Yuma found themselves fighting their former

The Knife

The knife was one of the most important tools of the Native American hunter or warrior, but it was not a weapon of preference. A warrior who had no alternative might use his knife to fight with, but might be better served by finding a rock to throw or a branch with which to strike his opponent – or perhaps beating a timely retreat and coming back properly armed.

Knives were typically of stone such as flint, flaked and knapped to create an extremely sharp edge, or of bone. Once high-quality metal blades became available in trade from Europeans, the traditional knife became much less common but could still be encountered from time to time. Handles were often of antler or a similar resilient material, and might be straight or curved to position the blade at an angle that suited the user.

Few warriors will have been specialist or even proficient knife-fighters; their efforts would be placed where they would be more generally useful such as learning woodcraft, marksmanship, horsemanship and fighting with hand weapons such as the spear or club.

The knife was very much a weapon of last resort for many, typically used to finish off a wounded enemy or in a rolling scramble on the ground after a fight had gone badly wrong. As such, its use in combat might better be considered as a 'killing tool' than a weapon as such.

Right: A Tlingit dagger, carved in similar manner to the wooden helmets used by Tlingit warriors. The knife was more of a tool than a weapon.

allies the Cocopah. Assistance came from the Mojave, forcing the Cocopah to agree peace terms. In turn, the Yuma and the Mojave came to an agreement with the troops at Fort Yuma that formed the basis of peaceful coexistence.

THE NEZ PERCÉ

The Nez Percé people, as they were misnamed by French explorers, were native to what is now Washington, Oregon, Idaho and Montana. They formed part of the Plateau Culture, occupying high land between mountain ranges in the northern USA and southern Canada. These tribes spoke languages from four different families – the Nez Percé shared close linguistic connections with the Cayuse and the Molala.

Dwelling between the Great Plains and the northwestern regions, the plateau people traded with both and were frequently visited by Chinook and other traders. They adopted concepts and habits from the tribes of other regions, such as the use by some tribes of headdresses to denote rank or great deeds. Not all the plateau tribes were receptive to new ideas, however.

Right: Warriors of the Nez Percé in full ceremonial dress. Some decoration was a personal choice, but other items had to be earned and awarded by the tribe.

The lifestyle was originally semi-nomadic, with the tribe moving to its permanent villages for the winter then spreading out to hunt in the summer. In the warmer months simple shelters were used and the tribe hunted a variety of game. In the winter much of the tribe's diet comprised fish caught in nearby watercourses; villages were usually situated to take advantage of good fishing conditions.

The Nez Percé, whose territory was on the eastern side of the plateau region and close to the Great Plains, acquired horses from

> *"...The Nez Percé gradually moved to a more nomadic lifestyle, using their mounts to travel out onto the plains to hunt buffalo."*

the Shoshone who lived to the south. The horse soon became so important to the tribe that they were noted for having more of them than even the Great Plains tribes. The Nez Percé gradually moved to a more nomadic lifestyle, using their mounts to travel out onto the plains to hunt buffalo.

Having achieved a dominant position in terms of both local politics and trade, the Nez Percé negotiated a treaty with the US government in the 1850s that guaranteed their ownership of most of their ancestral lands. This treaty was amended in 1863 to greatly reduce the size of their reservation, largely due

Above: The name 'Nez Percé' given to the tribe by French explorers is a misnomer; few tribe members actually possessed nose piercings.

Facing page: Chief Joseph was a great war leader but most of all he was an eloquent and persuasive diplomat who campaigned tirelessly on behalf of his people.

to the discovery of gold nearby. Escalating tensions quickly led to what became known as the Nez Percé War.

THE NEZ PERCÉ WAR

War was perhaps inevitable at some point, but the conflict was triggered in June 1876 when a white settler – who was known for his hatred of the nearby tribe – accused members of a Nez Percé hunting party of stealing horses from his land. Accounts of how the ensuing scuffle progressed are confused and contradictory, but the outcome was that a hunter – a friend of Nez Percé chief Joseph – was shot and killed. The horses were subsequently found wandering on the owner's land.

The local US authorities tried to reduce tensions, and in general agreed that the incident had been a deliberate murder for which the horses' owner should stand trial. Nothing was done, however, and eventually some elements of the Nez Percé lost patience. This was for the most part young men who

were spoiling for a fight and not inclined to listen when their chiefs urged caution.

The action taken by the Nez Percé was quite moderate. Messengers went to the homes of settlers in the area, summoning

"A deadline of one week was set, but the settlers began forming a militia and obviously intended to fight."

Below: Although innocent of the original charge that they had stolen settlers' horses, warriors of the Nez Percé later carried out raids which increased tensions.

them to a meeting where those who attended were instructed to hand over the murderers and leave the region. A deadline of one week was set, but the settlers began forming a militia and obviously intended to fight. The US cavalry force based nearby refused to assist them and instead sent troops to the area to try to keep the potential combatants apart.

Negotiations between the cavalry and the Nez Percé were successful, despite the fact that

Chief Joseph and his men were armed for war. They agreed to move away from the settlers and to avoid conflict if the murderers were tried for their crime. They were, but the charges were dismissed.

To resolve the tension between the settlers and the Nez Percé, the US government set up a commission, which decided – despite a strong case made by Chief Joseph – that the Nez Percé should be moved to a reservation. They refused to go, continuing to make representations to the effect that they should be permitted to remain in their ancestral home, and eventually the US government decided to remove them by force if they did not relocate. The Nez Percé agreed, but some of their warriors began raiding the settlers, and this brought about the conflict Chief Joseph had hoped to avoid.

The US response began with about 100 cavalry plus some civilian volunteers and Native American scouts who approached the Nez Percé as they were encamped at White Bird Canyon,

Idaho. The Nez Percé were not accustomed to fighting white men and had few guns, but they were superb horsemen with excellent mounts while the better-armed cavalry were inexperienced and poorly trained. They were also riding mounts that had not received proper cavalry training. The result was a rout for the US forces, largely through the panic of their horses.

CANADA BOUND

After the battle at White Bird Canyon, the Nez Percé began heading for Canada after first seeking – and being refused – refuge with the Crow. Greater US forces were mobilized against them, including many troops with Civil War experience, against whom the Nez Percé could only fight a rearguard action as

their tribe moved away from its ancestral homes. This action was generally successful, although the odds against the tribe were very steep.

After a series of skirmishes and mobile counterattacks made to slow the pursuit, the Nez Percé were under the leadership of Chief Looking Glass; Joseph's influence had diminished. They were in some cases able to pass peaceably through the lands of white settlers, which made the Nez Percé think they had outrun pursuit and could proceed to Canada in relative safety.

In August 1877, they were surprised as they camped at Big Hole in Montana. Serious casualties were suffered among warriors and noncombatants alike, as the US troops had orders not to take prisoners or enter into a

Above: The initial US cavalry force was inexperienced and easily defeated, but soon the Nez Percé found themselves facing large numbers of veteran troops.

parlay. As resistance firmed up the troops pulled back and deployed an artillery piece, whose crew were quickly shot down by Nez Percé marksmen. The warriors exchanged fire with US soldiers for the remainder of the day while the tribe retreated to a safer position, and the next day a handful of warriors kept the enemy pinned down with accurate fire at anyone who ventured out of his rifle pit.

The battle at Big Hole was a victory for the Nez Percé, who were able to break contact with an enemy force no longer in a condition to pursue them. However, it was apparent that they had not escaped – more soldiers would be coming, and the tribe was forced to continue its progress towards Canada.

After further skirmishes and rearguard actions the tribe camped at Bears Paw Mountain in late September 1877. Chief Joseph was once more leading the tribe, which was in a desperate state as a result of hardships and losses in the four-month retreat. There in Montana

the tribe was located by around 500 US troops accompanied by Cheyenne and Lakota scouts.

As the US attack developed, some of the Nez Percé attempted to flee towards the Canadian

> ## "*Warriors crept out at night to scavenge weapons, ammunition and food from casualties, and the battle became a siege.*"

border. Most of the tribe began an orderly movement as they had done repeatedly in the past, and the remaining warriors deployed to fight a rearguard action. The Cheyenne and Lakota scouts were more interested in capturing the Nez Percé horse herd than getting involved in a fight, but other elements of the force went straight at the encampment in the hope of overrunning it quickly. Instead they ran into rifle fire from warriors concealed in front of the camp.

Facing page: After an incident with a party of settlers at Birch Creek, Nez Percé warriors raided the pursuing force's pickets. The ensuing pursuit was ambushed at Camas Meadows.

Below: Chief Joseph negotiated a surrender on the best terms he could get, but the US government did not honour its agreement and inflicted further suffering on the Nez Percé.

Mass Communications

Above: Interrupting the smoke column to create distinct puffs of smoke allowed prearranged messages to be sent, conveying specific information to everyone who understood the code.

While a rider on a fast horse could carry a message over a very long distance in a short time, he could only be in one place. If he failed to locate the recipient of the message or was forced to waste time chasing down a dispersed party or tribe to pass on his news, lengthy delays became likely. One answer to this problem was to use smoke signals.

Smoke signals were produced by placing damp grass in a fire. The amount of information that could be conveyed was limited of course, but by prearranged codes a set of messages could be sent. Smoke from a particular hill, or smoke at a particular point on the hill, would have a meaning that only the sender and intended recipients would understand. Patterns could also be created by interrupting the production of smoke to create a simple code. By this means a tribe could quickly pass on a message – such as an alert of danger – to everyone nearby.

The initial attack was repulsed, but as the rest of the US force moved up the Nez Percé became surrounded. With no alternative they dug in, as did their enemies. Warriors crept out at night to scavenge weapons, ammunition and food from casualties, and the battle became a siege. An attempted parlay resulted in Chief Joseph being taken hostage, but he was exchanged for a US officer who allowed himself to be caught and so the siege continued.

The Nez Percé considered a breakout attempt, but while their warriors might have been able to manage it their wounded and most of the families would have to be left behind. This was unacceptable and with his people surrounded, starving and freezing without blankets, Chief Joseph agreed to surrender in return for a promise that his people could return home and go onto their reservation.

This promise was not kept. Instead the Nez Percé were sent to Indian Territory in Oklahoma for several years before finally being permitted to return home. Chief Joseph, who had won widespread admiration for his leadership of an almost 1200-mile fighting retreat, was not permitted to join them. He lived out his remaining days in Washington State.

THE NATIVE AMERICAN WARRIOR

The Native American warrior was not a soldier in the European sense, but he was capable of operating in an organized fashion

Below: Shooting from horseback without stirrups was a little easier than using a bow, but a high degree of horsemanship was still required to avoid wasting ammunition.

Sign Language

Above: Sign language had what might be termed different dialects, but was generally intuitive enough for strangers to figure out what someone wanted to convey.

A common sign language was used by many tribes, with gestures retaining their meaning even where spoken languages were quite different. Sign language might have offered the advantage of being able to communicate silently while sneaking up on prey animals or waiting to ambush an enemy, although in all probability it was mostly used as a supplement to verbal communication as its gestures tended to be intuitive to anyone in the habit of 'talking with their hands'.

For example, the sign for abandoning an endeavour resembled throwing an object on the ground with both hands in a sharp gesture of exasperation. Similar gestures are used today among people who cannot possibly have encountered plains sign language. It could help reduce misunderstandings where speakers of different dialects or languages from the same family were trying to communicate. It could make at least simple communication possible between groups that had no common language, and was often intelligible – to some degree at least – by Europeans who spoke no native languages.

and carrying out complex tactics. His mode of warfare was largely about people rather than terrain objectives – killing enemies was no more or less useful than making them realize they could not come into the tribe's lands with impunity or that they must move elsewhere. Land was used but not owned in the sense that the white settlers understood it, which was one reason for conflict.

The warrior was capable of what might be termed great savagery, but he was not cruel for the sake of it – or at least, most individuals were not. This was a harsh and unforgiving world with few second chances; and, like many indigenous peoples, the Native American warrior lived close to nature. Nature simply does not care who or what lives or dies; there are predators and there are prey, and nature takes its course. So it was in the Americas – a strong and warlike tribe could choose whether to live in peace or to go on the warpath, whereas a weaker tribe might not be given the choice.

Conditions changed rapidly in the 500 years or so after Europeans arrived in the Americas, and the Native American warrior adapted. His skill at hunting in the woodlands with a bow translated almost effortlessly to skirmishing with a musket or rifle in the same terrain. The hunt for bison or even mammoth on the plains was made easier and more efficient by the adoption of the horse and the gun, but hunter and prey remained largely the same. The conflicts fought by these warriors were not,

as a certain genre of movies might have us believe, between the white man and the Native American. Instead they were fought between a particular tribe or a segment of that tribe and whomever they happened to be fighting at the time. The politics of the North American continent were complex and sometimes violent before Europeans arrived. Once they entered the mix, a new dimension emerged, but there was never a simple 'us and them' situation with just two sides.

> "The warrior was capable of what might be termed great savagery, but was not cruel for the sake of it – or at least, most individuals were not."

Nor was the Native American warrior a helpless victim of the 'white man'. Tribes dealt with groups of settlers as suited their own agendas, and used the early settlers in their wars as often as they were used by them. The response of some tribes to the arrival of Europeans – such as fighting wars to control trade – had a greater impact than the Europeans themselves.

Over time, the situation did polarize, but other than in the minds of 'Indian-haters' there was no all-encompassing war between two cultures. The expanding United States came into conflict with one tribe or confederation then another as interests clashed. Conflict was rarely sought, but

Right: Men of the Canadian Cree pictured in 1916, during World War I. The eldest generation – at front – saw their grandsons born into a completely changed world.

when it came it was savage. The Native American warrior acquitted himself admirably in these wars; at the end of the 19th century he was still inflicting painful defeats on much larger forces fielded by an emerging world power.

The warriors of the Native American tribes may or may not have realized at the time that they were fighting for their way of life. On some occasions, such as when resisting religious conversion or an attempt to outlaw traditional

> *"The Native American tribes produced some of the finest fighting men the world has ever seen, led by clever and innovative commanders."*

practices, it would have seemed so. At other times they fought for their land, their tribe, for vengeance against an enemy who had wronged them or for plunder and glory.

The Native American tribes produced some of the finest fighting men the world has ever seen, led by clever and innovative commanders. Their eclipse marks a turning point in military history – courage and skill never went out of fashion, but warfare was increasingly dominated by logistics and industrial capability. Less than 25 years after the end of the 'Indian Wars', World War I broke out. Warfare had changed completely by then, and the warrior had been completely supplanted by the soldier.

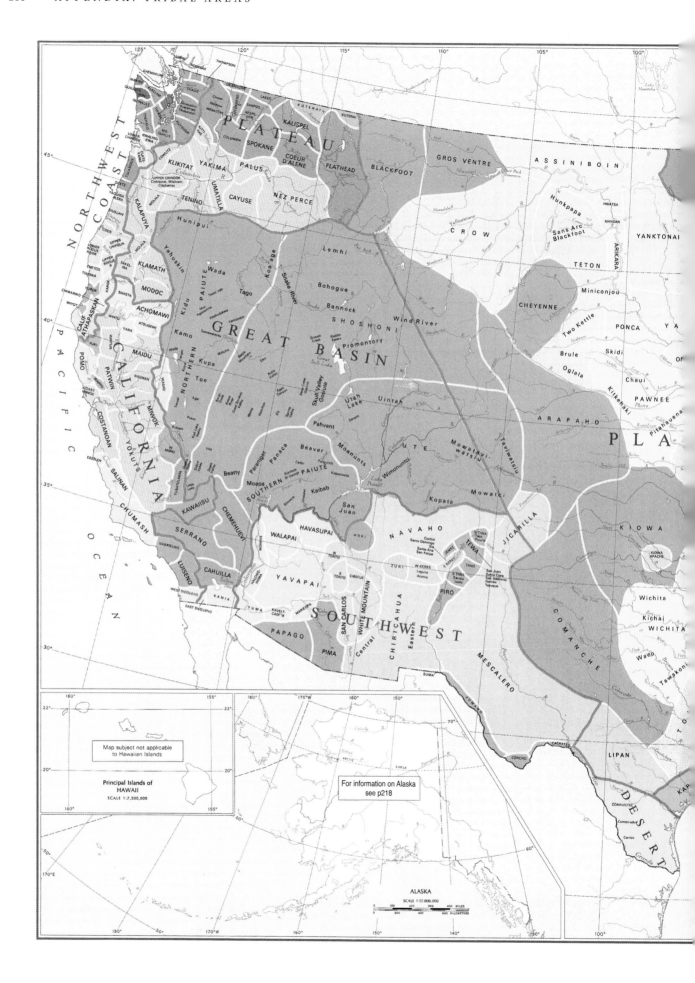

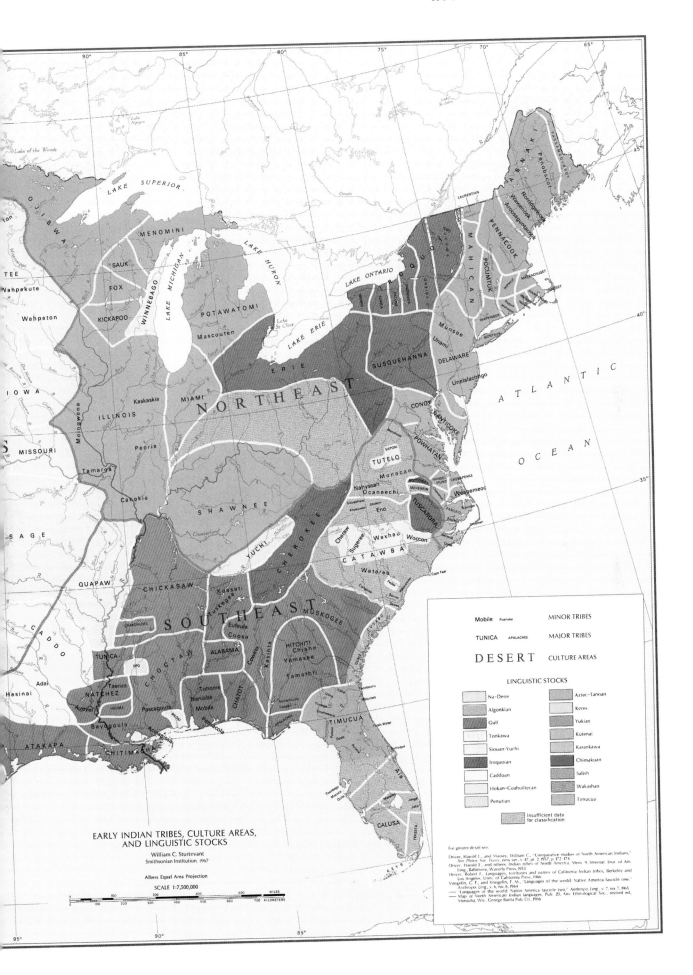

EARLY INDIAN TRIBES, CULTURE AREAS,
AND LINGUISTIC STOCKS

William C. Sturtevant
Smithsonian Institution, 1967

Albers Equal Area Projection

SCALE 1:7,500,000

Mobile   Roanoke   MINOR TRIBES

TUNICA   APALACHEE   MAJOR TRIBES

DESERT   CULTURE AREAS

LINGUISTIC STOCKS

Na-Dene   Aztec-Tanoan

Algonkian   Keres

Gulf   Yukian

Tonkawa   Kutenai

Siouan-Yuchi   Karankawa

Iroquoian   Chimakuan

Caddoan   Salish

Hokan-Coahuiltecan   Wakashan

Penutian   Timucua

Insufficient data
for classification

For greater detail see:

Driver, Harold E., and Massey, William C. "Comparative studies of North American Indians."
   Am. Philos. Soc. Trans., new ser., v. 47, pt. 2, 1957, p. 172-174.
Driver, Harold E. and others, Indian tribes of North America. Mem. 9, Internat. Jour. of Am.
   Ling., Baltimore, Waverly Press, 1953.
Heizer, Robert F. Languages, territories and names of California Indian tribes, Berkeley and
   Los Angeles, Univ. of California Press, 1966.
Voegelin, C. F., and Voegelin, F. M., "Languages of the world: Native America fascicle one."
   Anthropo. Ling., v. 6, no. 6, 1964.
—— "Languages of the world: Native America fascicle two." Anthropo. Ling., v. 7, no. 7, 1965.
—— Map of North American Indian languages. Pub. 20, Am. Ethnological Soc., revised ed.,
   Menasha, Wis., George Banta Pub. Co., 1966.

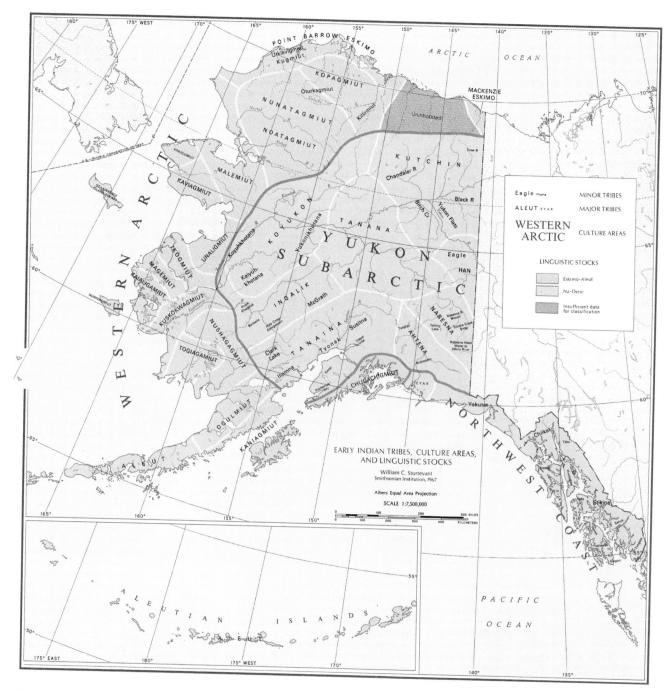

EARLY INDIAN TRIBES, CULTURE AREAS,
AND LINGUISTIC STOCKS

William C. Sturtevant
Smithsonian Institution, 1967

Albers Equal Area Projection

SCALE 1:7,500,000

Native American society was complex, with multiple strata. Typically, several extended families made up a band, and several bands formed a tribe, which might be part of a large confederacy. Attempts to map the territory of these tribes and confederacies are at best general, since to many tribes there was only 'the land we currently use' rather than any clearly defined territorial boundaries.

The tribal distributions on this map are arbitrary at many points. Detailed knowledge of tribal areas was acquired at different times in different regions. For example, by the time knowledge was gained of the areas occupied by the Plains tribes, many groups in the east had become extinct or moved location.

Genetic relationships between languages are also shown on the maps based on studies published in the 1960s.

Source: National Atlas of the United States of America – Department of the Interior, U.S. Geological Survey, Reston, Virginia

INDEX

PICTURE CREDITS